Practice
Energy Healing
in *Integrity*

The Joy of Offering Your Gifts
Legally & Ethically

Midge Murphy, JD, PhD
(Energy Medicine)

PROFESSIONAL LIABILITY RISK
MANAGEMENT CONSULTANT

ETHICS AND LEGAL PRINCIPLES IN THE
PRACTICE OF ENERGY HEALING METHODS

ENERGY HEALING PRACTITIONER

TERRITORIAL PUBLISHING

EUGENE, OREGON

Disclaimer

The information contained in this book is for instructional and educational purposes only and is not legal or ethical advice or opinion. Further, the information contained in this book is provided only as general information, which may or may not reflect the most current legal and ethical developments. This information is not provided in the course of an attorney-client relationship and is not intended to constitute legal advice or opinion, or to substitute for obtaining legal or risk management advice from a professional.

Practice Energy Healing in Integrity
The Joy of Offering Your Gifts Legally & Ethically
© 2015–2020 Midge Murphy

Printed in the United States of America
Cover Design: Claire Last
Special thanks to Patricia Marshall and Luminare Press
for their help with interior and cover design and layout

Territorial Publishing
82985 Territorial Hwy.
Eugene, OR 97405
www.midgemurphy.com

ISBN: 978-0-9904875-1-7

LCCN: 2015913278

This book is dedicated to the hummingbird,
who sings a magical song of
pure joy, healing, manifestation, and accomplishment

Contents

Introduction

WELCOME! SINCE THIS BOOK WAS first published in 2015 the practice of energy healing methods has continued to grow. Now in 2020, it's time to update and expand the book to include additional essential content for my readers. I am gratified and honored that this book and the Exam based on this book have been recognized as the national ethics standard by the National Certification Center of Energy Practitioners. As with the first version, I'm pleased to offer you this updated and expanded comprehensive book designed to assist you in understanding the core ethical issues and related legal principles in the practice of energy healing methods. Over the many years that I've been advising practitioners and organizations about legal issues in the practice of energy healing methods, many initially are resistant to anything legal. It's not uncommon for clients to remark that dealing with legalities feels "off-putting", "harsh", "scary", and even incongruent to being a compassionate practitioner. What I've experienced is that once legal issues are addressed and appropriate risk management strategies are implemented, the client moves from a place of fear to one of empowerment. Being empowered allows you to practice in integrity and experience the joy of offering your energy healing gifts legally and ethically.

Energy healing methods include a broad spectrum of techniques, therapies, and approaches, including Therapeutic Touch, Healing Touch, Reiki, chakra balancing, Eden Energy Medicine, meridian tapping techniques such as Emotional Freedom Techniques (EFT), and many others. Since many energy healing methods are based on the new emerging fields of energy medicine and energy psychology, they are considered experimental by the mainstream health care industry, the legal system, licensing boards, and regulatory agencies. Consequently, all practitioners who use energy healing methods, whether licensed or non-licensed, face significant legal risks. Therefore, this book also provides you with essential risk management strategies intended to help protect your practice from the potential legal liabilities inherent in offering energy healing methods to the public.

In addition to learning about the overarching ethical framework, you will have the opportunity to identify the potential ethical and/or legal vulnerabilities that could be present in your practice. You will have the opportunity to learn how to assess and select appropriate clients to work with. You will also be introduced to the core ethical concepts in therapeutic relationships and how they apply to energy healing practitioners. From that foundation you will be able to expand the traditional view of ethics to include working with clients on intuitive and energetic levels. In defining a new ethic of caring with clients, this book also explores the concept of the therapeutic relationship as a sacred contract between the practitioner and client. This sacred contract utilizes archetypes as the guardians of ethical relationships. You will discover creating a legally sound and ethical practice is based on a number of components, including:

- Being competently and professionally trained.
- Appropriately assessing and selecting clients.
- Doing your own healing work.
- Having your own personal code of ethics.
- Following professional ethics codes.
- Implementing appropriate risk management strategies.
- Complying with applicable laws and regulations.

Energy healing methods fall under the umbrella of Complementary and Alternative Medicine (CAM), which is defined as a consensus term for healing methods, techniques, processes, and systems that have historically fallen outside established, recognized Western medicine. CAM methods are considered *complementary* or *alternative* healing arts in the United States. CAM includes both licensed healing arts practitioners such as chiropractors and non-licensed alternative healing arts practitioners such as Reiki practitioners. Therefore, CAM methods fall into two categories, those that are regulated by state licensing laws and those that are not regulated. Chiropractic medicine is regulated in all fifty states in that chiropractors must be licensed in order to practice. There are other CAM methods that are regulated in some states but not in other states. These states require nutritionists (i.e. registered dietitians), massage therapists, naturopathic physicians, and acupuncturists to be licensed in order to practice. There are a multitude of unregulated CAM methods, including Reiki, Healing Touch, the Emotion Code/Body Code, EFT/Tapping, and shamanism. For the purposes of this book, when I refer to energy healing methods, I am referring to unregulated CAM methods. Ethical conduct is vital to the integrity, authenticity, and acceptance of CAM methods and energy healing practitioners as they participate in the larger health care and wellness industries.

While the information contained in this book is based on U.S. laws and regulations, readers who reside outside the U.S. will find the ethical principles and much of the risk management strategies discussed of value no matter where they practice. In addition, even if you only use energy healing methods with friends and family, this information will enhance your use of such methods with your loved ones.

The information contained in this book is not intended to raise concerns but to broaden your knowledge base, to help empower you to practice in integrity so you can provide the highest ethical service to your clients, and to provide you with valuable risk management strategies and tools so you can experience the joy of offering your energy healing gifts legally and ethically.

Section I

Legal & Regulatory System That Governs Helping Professions

IT'S IMPERATIVE FOR PRACTITIONERS WHO use energy healing methods with clients to have an understanding of the legal and regulatory system that governs helping professionals. This understanding provides the platform for practitioners to be able to deliver energy healing in integrity. It's also imperative for practitioners to know how the innovative energy healing methods they use with clients fit into the current health care field. This is essential in order for practitioners to experience the joy of offering their services within a legally sound and ethical energy healing practice. In this first section, we consider the realities that apply to all practitioners of innovative energy-oriented systems of healing and transformation. Like all pioneers, energy healing practitioners face many challenges. Issues that must be confronted are:

- Defining their place within Complementary and Alternative Medicine (CAM).
- Interfacing with the regulatory agencies that are helping to shape the future of CAM.
- Gaining acceptance and validation by the mainstream health care industry.
- Understanding how to create a legally sound and ethical practice.

- Implementing risk management strategies and tools to protect their practices.
- Creating an ethic of caring that includes working with a client's energy field.

This book encompasses these issues but also addresses the need for a deeper understanding of the ethic of caring in the therapeutic relationship between practitioner and client. This ethic of caring in a therapeutic relationship prompts us to expand our view of ethics to include the subtleties of working within the human energy field. Section VII will explore in depth the concept of the therapeutic relationship as a sacred contract between the practitioner and client This will include the use of archetypes as guardians of ethical relationships.

Energy healing methods are being used by many types of healing professionals, both licensed and non-licensed. Traditional licensed health care providers such as physicians, nurses, physical therapists, psychologists and other mental health care professionals are now incorporating energy healing methods into their respective practices. Professionals using energy healing methods also include practitioners who are licensed in some states but not in others, such as massage therapists, naturopaths, dieticians, and acupuncturists. A third group of practitioners using energy healing methods that are currently not subject to licensure includes energy healing practitioners, EFT/Tapping practitioners, pastoral/spiritual counselors, medical intuitives, life coaches, shamans, and many others.

Historical development of licensing statutes and regulations

It's IMPORTANT TO KNOW THAT under the Tenth Amendment to the U.S. Constitution each state has the right to pass laws and regulations to protect the safety and welfare of its citizens. Other countries also have similar laws. A primary method of safeguarding the health and well-being of citizens is to license professions to ensure that basic levels of education, competency, and skills are established and maintained. All fifty states have medical and psychology practice acts, as well as other types of practice acts including, social workers, chiropractors, and nurses. A violation of these laws can result in the criminal charge of practicing a licensed profession without a license.

Over the past 100 years these medical licensing statutes have been construed broadly by the legal system resulting in courts finding that just about any type of healing work is considered the practice of medicine. This finding has occurred if the practitioner is addressing physical issues with a client. For example, courts have historically affirmed convictions of "laying-on-of-hands" healers for unlawfully practicing medicine. Psychotherapy licensing statutes have also been construed broadly resulting in courts finding that just about any kind of emotional work is considered the practice of psychotherapy. This finding has occurred if the practitioner is addressing emotional issues with a client. Thus, the legal paradigm mirrors Biomedicine's historical view that alternative practices, such as energy healing methods, are deviant, suspect, or "on the fringe." Therefore, a non-licensed energy healing practitioner faces the risk of being charged with the crime of practicing a licensed profession such as medicine or psychotherapy without a license.

Even though research is beginning to support the safety and efficacy of energy healing methods, they are still considered "unsubstantiated methods" by licensing boards, regulatory agencies, and the courts. Currently, no energy healing method has been determined to have passed the "gold standard" of being accepted as an evidence-based therapy. As an example, a physician who uses an energy healing method, such as Therapeutic Touch for helping patients recover more quickly from surgery, may face a malpractice claim and be subject to professional discipline for using an unsubstantiated method that has not yet met the evidence-based standard. This situation could result in the suspension or loss of the physician's license. In such a case, what is helpful for the physician to know is that although Therapeutic Touch has not been fully accepted as an evidence-based therapy, there is valid scientific research indicating that Therapeutic Touch meets the criteria to be considered an evidenced-supported therapy. The physician can also demonstrate that there are a substantial number of allied licensed practitioners such as nurses using Therapeutic Touch. Also, the physician can provide research demonstrating that Therapeutic Touch has been shown to be beneficial to a substantial number of patients. In addition, Therapeutic Touch has an international organization that has developed standards of practice and credentialing for Therapeutic Touch practitioners (Therapeutic Touch International Association). Under the "respectable minority" legal doctrine, the physician could use all of this information to defend a claim from the physician's licensing board for using an unsubstantiated therapy that falls below the standard of care. It's likely that the physician would prevail under the respectable minority doctrine, if the physician's licensing board charged the physician with unprofessional conduct for using an energy healing method such as Therapeutic Touch. However, if the physician were to use an energy healing method without being able to demonstrate that a respectable minority of competent doctors also use it, then the physician would not meet the criteria to assert the respectable minority defense. In such a case, the physician's licensing board could subject the physician to professional discipline for practicing below the standards of care and outside the scope of practice for using an unsubstantiated therapy; thereby putting the physician's license to practice medicine at risk.

A unique feature of many energy healing methods is that they can be used in a variety of contexts, depending on the legally defined scope of practice of the practitioner. They can be used for mental health issues, physical symptoms, life coaching, stress management, peak performance, spiritual counseling, as a self-help tool, and to support the body's natural ability to heal. For example, meridian tapping techniques can be used within a psychotherapeutic setting with professional mental health care clinicians who are fully trained in meridian tapping. Another example is that Healing Touch can be incorporated into an allied health care practice such as a physical therapy practice for pain management. A massage therapist may use Reiki to help a client deeply relax thereby enhancing the effectiveness of the massage. Energy healing methods can also be used as self-help techniques and shared with family members and friends.

> Therefore, in what context a practitioner uses energy healing methods with clients will indicate how that particular practitioner's practice fits within the current legal and regulatory system that governs healing arts practitioners.

> Some energy healing practitioners may feel that these licensing laws are unfair, overbearing, and restrictive. However, there is a reasonable basis for why things are the way they are.
> We can all agree that the safety and welfare of our clients is paramount. The underlying regulatory value for licensing laws is to protect the safety and welfare of citizens.

Definition of Complementary & Alternative Medicine (CAM) & Energy Medicine

THERE IS NO UNIVERSALLY ACCEPTED definition of CAM. Michael H. Cohen, in his groundbreaking book entitled *Future Medicine: Ethical Dilemmas, Regulatory Challenges, and Therapeutic Pathways to Health Care and Healing in Human Transformation* (2003), defines CAM as a consensus term for healing therapies that have historically fallen outside established, recognized biomedicine. He goes on to explain that CAM methods have been classified into at least eight major fields of practice:

- Mind/body interventions, including, yoga, prayer, mental healing, psycho-sensory methods, and energy modalities.

- Bioelectromagnetic applications in medicine.
- Alternative systems of medical practice, including traditional Oriental medicine and acupuncture, Ayurveda, homeopathy, and Native American medicine.
- Manual healing methods, including massage, somatic therapies, and chiropractic.
- Pharmacological and biological treatments not yet accepted by mainstream medicine
- Herbal medicine, also including phytomedicine.
- Treatments focusing on diet and nutrition in the prevention and treatment of chronic diseases.
- Energy Medicine and Energy Psychology, EFT/Tapping and Cognitive-Somatic Energy Practices.

Cohen defines Energy Medicine as that "subset of therapies within the spectrum of complementary and alternative medical therapies that primarily are based on the projection of information, consciousness, and/or intentionality to the patient," (Cohen, 2003, p.9). He identifies Energy Psychology, meridian tapping techniques, medical intuition, Therapeutic Touch, Healing Touch, Reiki, Oriental medicine, distance healing, and many other related modalities as examples of Energy Medicine. Further, he writes, "energy therapies are sometimes known by specific modalities and techniques such as laying-on-of-hands, intuitive medical diagnosis and distance healing, and aspects of traditional oriental medicine, Tibetan medicine, and herbal medicine, all come under the rubric of Energy Medicine. The thrust is an understanding of medicine and healing that incorporates and simultaneously transcends the physical world as presently understood, including known biological, chemical, pharmacological, and other mechanisms in our human anatomy and physiology." Therefore, under Cohen's definition, energy healing methods would fall within several categories including Mind/body interventions, Manual healing methods, Energy Medicine and Energy Psychology.

Defining appropriate ethical conduct for energy-oriented practitioners requires innovation and a willingness to think well beyond the usual therapeutic parameters of non-harming with a client-centered orientation. Because energy healing practitioners are developing their practices within a major paradigm shift, it's essential to expand their thinking to include areas such as the healthy use of intuited material, addressing emotional issues that spontaneously arise with energy healing methods, and holding exquisite clarity about boundaries.

National overview of Complementary & Alternative Medicine (CAM)

In recent years, CAM has become more widely used and is becoming socially and politically more accepted in the United States. Given this trend, the federal government has established within the National Institutes of Health, the Office of Complementary and Alternative Medicine to study and research various CAM methods and products. Under President Clinton, the White House convened a commission to study CAM. As a result, the National Academies, Institute of Medicine, concluded that it is important to explore and understand the scientific and policy implications of CAM use by the American public. In January 2003, the Institute of Medicine convened a committee to explore scientific, policy and practice questions that arise from the significant and increasing use of CAM methods by the American public. Specifically, the committee was asked to identify major scientific and policy issues in the following four areas:

- CAM research and challenges and needs.
- CAM regulation in the United States and other countries.
- Interface and integration of CAM with conventional medicine.
- Training and certification questions of CAM practitioners.

Because CAM methods are, for the most part, still considered outside of mainstream health care, ethical conduct by CAM practitioners is essential to the acceptance of CAM methods. The results of the study "Complementary and Alternative Medicine in the United States," have been published by the National Academies Press and can be ordered at www.nap.edu.

Overview of energy healing methods in the United States; the National Certification Center of Energy Practitioners

MANY OF MY COLLEAGUES DEFINE the current state of the practice of energy healing methods in the United States as the "wild, wild, West." This is because, as previously stated, the field is unregulated and anyone can claim the title of an energy healing practitioner. It's not uncommon for someone to hang a shingle as an energy healing practitioner after taking only a weekend workshop, by reading a book, or reviewing training material over the Internet. Many of these energy healing practitioners have good intentions in starting a practice, usually because they have had a positive outcome from using energy healing methods and want to help others. I honor their desire to offer energy healing services. However, it's imperative to understand wanting to "heal" people does not create a legally sound and ethical practice. Having a professional practice is a business that has a number of components and requires an investment of time and money. Practitioners not only need to commit time and money in obtaining proper training in the energy healing methods of their choice, but they also must budget for office space, marketing costs, and risk management services.

Under existing licensure statutes governing healing arts professionals in the United States, it's not possible to become licensed as an energy healing practitioner. However, many states and the federal government have requested that the field of energy healing establish national standards and a framework for testing and qualifying energy healing practitioners. Otherwise, the states would begin licensing energy healing practitioners in a manner similar to other licensed health care professions. A few states such as Massachusetts have already attempted to pass legislation requiring energy healing practitioners to be licensed in order to practice. As a result, in 2018, the ***National Alliance of Energy Practitioners*** was formed as a coalition comprised of most of the major associations and training programs in the field of energy healing (NAOEP). The purpose of the NAOEP is to share information about quality energy healing practices, educate the public on the styles of energy work, their use, the research on energy healing practices, and the limits of what a professional energy healing practitioner can do. Because some states are already attempting to require licensure for energy healing practitioners, the NAOEP realized that it was urgent to establish self-regulation in the field. The consensus was that it's not a good idea to leave it up to the states to decide licensure requirements for energy healing practitioners.

Also, in 2018 the ***National Certification Center of Energy Practitioners*** (NCCOEP) was formed as a sister organization to the NAOEP. The mission of the NCCOEP is to act as a professional testing organization that develops, supports, and promotes national standards for energy healing practitioners. The NCCOEP also includes ethics and standards of practice for energy healing practitioners. The NCCOEP has followed the example of the Acupuncture community in creating national quality standards and a national testing process to certify energy healing practitioners in the United States. Currently the NCCOEP has twelve different divisions and accepts applications to become certified from a broad spectrum of energy healing practitioners. While there are several entry points for becoming certified by the NCCOEP, the predominant way is by receiving certification from an NAOEP member organization that trains energy healing practitioners in a specific energy healing method.

One of the long-term goals of the NAOEP is to establish trade organizations in every state. These trade organizations would provide the states with the means for licensing energy healing practitioners. So instead of the state deciding specific licensure requirements, the state would look to the trade organization and require that the energy healing practitioner be certified by the NCCOEP in order to practice.

Section II

Key Ethical Principles for Energy Healing Practitioners

Within the context of the growing dimension of complementary health care, this section explores key ethical principles that directly relate to your individual endeavor as an energy healing practitioner. It also explores the impact of being innovators in a new field and the potential ethical vulnerabilities that could be present in your practice. A fully developed ethical framework for working with clients in your energy healing practice is based on a number of components, including being client-centered, respecting your client's values, doing your own healing work, and developing your own personal code of ethics.

The need for an ethical framework for the practice of energy healing methods

Ethics is at the very heart of human caring and the foundation for creating the highest levels of professionalism for practitioners of the healing arts. It is the springboard for the many theories, philosophies, and activities that are foundational to the health care professions. The intention to reach out to someone in need arises out of an internal imperative to be genuine, helpful, and truthful in our interactions with others. This intention of caring requires careful nurturing to bring skillful awareness to every choice we make. This intention mandates careful interactions with others to ensure that our transactions are of the highest integrity and in keeping with our values so there is congruency.

The quality of such integrity is highly personal and entails maturity and wisdom to blossom into its unique manifestation in each practitioner. Understandably, it is challenging to delineate our essential values in brief terms, to make them practical, and to develop our ideals so that we can speak of them with directness. At our best, we would each have an actual working personal philosophy of caring or a personal code of ethics. To begin formulating a personal code of ethics for your energy healing practice, a helpful process is to perform a core values assessment. You will have the opportunity to do this exercise and examine your core values as an energy healing practitioner at the end of this Section. We may think of synonyms for ethical behaviors by saying they are actions that are decent, honorable, honest, virtuous, equitable, just, appropriate, and right for the situation at hand. Ethical actions align us with our highest principles and values on behalf of our clients to help them achieve their fullest potential. To help maintain the quality and effectiveness of an ethical relationship, it's essential to set the intention to be fully present and centered during a session with a client. Also, when we are fully present and centered, we are better able to ensure that our own issues are not being triggered or influencing our ability to make the best ethical choices when working with clients.

A FOUNDATIONAL STRUCTURE FOR AN ethical practice can be organized into three central aspects of an ethic of caring. One is the dimension of caring for clients as captured in the repeated wish to be client-centered, to do what is best for them, and to offer them the best possible resources. Another dimension is that of developing positive, healthy relationships with our professional communities, our local environments, and the public by "speaking our truth" to colleagues and others. A third dimension is to establish an ongoing personal awareness – knowing one's strengths and liabilities, doing what is right in a given situation and aligning with the spiritual dimension to connect with our highest ideals. It also includes acknowledging and being aware of those forces we may not be fully conscious of that psychology calls the "darker" or "shadow" side of the personality.

As the dimensions involve establishing and developing healthy, mindful relationships, there is a need to create ethical relationships in each of the three aspects. One image that may provide insight to the quality of an ethical relationship is the presence of our own energetic core. In Eastern Indian traditions, the *shushumna* is the central energetic line that flows from the top of the head to the base of the spine and supports the flow of the vital life force, or prana. When we are in harmony with the central core of our being, imaged as this straight energetic line, we are at one with ourselves and the world around us. However, a single event, word, gesture, or negative intention can throw us off, putting us out of balance. Fortunately, we can develop skills that can put us back into alignment with ourselves so we are balanced and aware of the needs of our clients and therefore can ethically be of service to them.

> Staying fully present and centered while working with a client is a *unique* and key ethical principle for all energy healing practitioners.

Definitions and key terms

THE ESSENTIAL PRINCIPLES OF HEALTH care ethics are:

- Autonomy – client's right to make a voluntary, knowing, and informed choice.
- Beneficence – practitioner's obligation to offer a benefit to a client.
- Do no harm.

The overall purpose of ethics is to guide professional practitioners so that clients' welfare remains the first priority. Simply put, ethical codes are conduct guidelines. Many energy healing methods are relatively new healing approaches and there are no existing universal conduct guidelines. Therefore, practitioners may inadvertently act unethically because they may not be aware of or have not considered all aspects of relevant issues. Expanding their grasp of ethical principles can help practitioners understand the impact of their behavior on clients and can provide knowledge and tools to act appropriately. It also allows practitioners to practice energy healing in integrity and provides them with the opportunity to experience the joy of offering their energy healing gifts legally and ethically.

The foundation for creating ethical codes in CAM and specifically energy healing methods can be found in various related health care fields such as medicine, psychology, and massage. While none of these fields operate in the same way as energy healing method's use of consciousness, intuition, and subtle energies, they provide a foundation for ethical behavior in a practice that incorporates energy healing methods.

When we begin to consider ethics, we may often use other terms such as values, morals, laws, integrity, principles, and professionalism interchangeably with ethics. While ethics is the study of moral philosophy, which encompasses all of these terms, they are not the same. For purposes of clarification, let's take a look at each of these fundamental terms.

- **Ethics** is the study of the general nature of morals and of the appropriate choices to be made by an individual in relationship with others. This can be expanded to include groups and professions. As such, ethics goes beyond what can be defined or codified in legal terms. Ethics deals with your moment-by-moment decision-making, especially when no one else is looking. Ethics in energy work involves personal healing and integrity, expertise in the modalities used with clients, working within the appropriate standards of practice and within one's legally defined scope of practice, complying with applicable laws and regulations, and treating the therapeutic relationship with clients as a sacred contract.

- **Values** are tangible and intangible beliefs that people consider to be part of their essential nature. Values are based on convictions and attitudes. For example, a core value for an energy healing practitioner may be to trust his intuition. In addition, respect and concern for others are two values deeply ingrained in health care professionals. Values may vary over our lifetime and will be different for each of us.

- **Principles** comprise our individual code of honor and create the framework for us to behave with integrity. Principles empower us to adapt our behavior so that each action arises from our core values and deeply held sense of self. Energy healing practitioners that hold the principle of compassion for their clients may be reflecting the value of being nonjudgmental in working with clients. As with values, principles will differ from one person to another.

- **Integrity** means adhering to an ethical code of behavior. It means a practitioner's behavior is congruent with his beliefs, principles, knowledge, intuition, and emotions. Integrity means there is harmony between different internal functions, such as our values, which result in external behavior that is consistent and ethical.

- **Morals** relate to a judgment of human actions and character. Morals are usually based on cultural or religious standards and may define what is considered "good" or "bad" behavior. Keep in mind that what is moral in one culture could be considered immoral by another.

- **Laws** are codified rules of conduct set forth by society and are generally based on shared ethical or moral principles. Laws are enforceable by the courts with the purpose of protecting the public's welfare. Laws and regulations are promulgated by the federal government, by states, and local municipalities. Practitioners must adhere to not only federal and state laws but also regulations set forth by licensing boards. In addition, there may be local municipal laws and regulations that affect your practice. For example, some cities do not allow energy healing practices to be operated from a home. Practitioners may also need a city or county business license in order to practice.

- **Professionalism** is the highest level of integrity a professional can convey to others. Professionalism emanates from your attitudes, values, and principles and is manifested through your practice. It includes your technical competency, your proficiency at communication skills, your respect and compassion, your skill at handling boundaries, and your business practices. Incorporating professionalism as part of your energy healing practice is equal to behaving ethically. Obviously, ethical violations are unprofessional. However, not all unprofessional behavior is considered unethical. For instance, dressing in torn workout clothes when working with a client is unprofessional, but it's not unethical.

Core ethical concepts in therapeutic relationships

THERE ARE A NUMBER OF core ethical concepts in therapeutic relationships that have been developed in the health care field to guide professional caregivers to behave responsibly and ethically. These concepts create the bedrock of ethical decision-making and responsible behavior in all professional helping relationships. The fundamental considerations for a therapeutic relationship are:

- To be client-centered.
- To maintain the fiduciary relationship and confidentiality.
- To develop a professional environment for structure and safety.
- To be sensitive to the power differential.
- To address transference and countertransference issues.
- To avoid dual relationships with clients.
- To obtain informed consent and disclose risks and benefits.

Client-centered care means the focus and purpose of all interventions is directed at the needs of the client, not the practitioner's desires, interests, or wishes. Without keen awareness, it's possible for the practitioner to violate this core ethical principle during a session by losing this focus. For example, if the client is a real estate broker and the practitioner asks for advice about selling a house, then the focus has shifted to the needs and interests of the practitioner instead of the client. *Client-centered care* also means that the client has a voice in the healing process and must agree to the nature and course of the work for it to proceed (informed consent). ***The client is considered a partner in the decision-making process.*** Considering the client as a partner in the healing process is a new orientation of ethics that is emerging with the growing use of CAM methods. The old model in Western medicine is more akin to an orientation where the doctor/patient relationship is hierarchal and paternalistic in nature and not a partnership. In addition, the practitioner has a commitment to create a space that is safe and supports and nurtures the client, allowing the inner wisdom of the client to be a full participant in the healing process.

The ethical principle of trust is a cornerstone for all helping professionals. Clients believe that the practitioner will be honest, not conceal any vital relevant information, and maintain the confidentiality of what is entrusted to the practitioner. Underlying all of these beliefs is the ethical principle of *fiduciary responsibility* (i.e. the trust the client places in their health care professional). All health care practitioners have a legally sanctioned fiduciary relationship with their clients. The fiduciary relationship requires practitioners to act in the best interests of a client. This sets a higher standard of responsible behavior and a legal requirement on the practitioner to ensure that client trust is maintained. Adherence to the fiduciary relationship helps remind practitioners that a client's well-being always remains the primary focus and minimizes the impact of any potential conflicts of interest. A violation of the fiduciary duty can result in legal liability. The issues of the fiduciary relationship become more pronounced in therapeutic relationships that involve energy healing methods. In many cases, the energy healing practitioner attunes to the client's needs not only verbally but intuitively and makes decisions based on information received in multi-dimensional ways.

Practitioners are ethically required to provide *a professional environment that is structured and safe.* The therapeutic relationship is set-up so that a specific time to meet is agreed upon in a professional environment, the length of each session is determined, and there is agreement on office procedures and payment requirements. Furthermore, the client has a right to expect that emotional, intellectual, physical, sexual, and energetic boundaries are honored. Thus, practitioners must create a safe, protected environment, free of inappropriate personal comments or sexual innuendos. In addition, many energy healing methods can result in a client experiencing an altered state of consciousness during a session. Clients can easily become disoriented, lightheaded, or "spacey" during and after an energy healing session. It's imperative for the practitioner to make sure the client is grounded and able to function before leaving the session. Otherwise, a disoriented client can be unstable both physically and emotionally. No practitioner wants to see a client fall or be injured leaving a session or experience a car accident or other kind of unfortunate incident after a session.

The *power differential* is inherent in any therapeutic relationship. The power in a therapeutic relationship is knowledge and skill. There are two kinds of power that create the power differential. The first is the practitioner's expertise and the presumption that the practitioner is knowledgeable and skilled at providing the healing services to the client. The second kind of power is once the therapeutic relationship is established the practitioner knows a lot more about the client than the client knows about the practitioner. In ethical practice, awareness of the power differential brings benefit by acknowledging that the client is in a more vulnerable position. The implicit acknowledgment of the practitioner's expertise is amplified by the physical, psychological, and intuitive aspects of energy healing methods. It's critical to ask yourself, how am I handling my power? The practitioner may be tempted to misuse the power and take advantage of the client, if the practitioner is not diligent about ethically maintaining the power differential. Awareness of the power differential between client and practitioner means sensitivity to the reality that clients often agree to any suggestion the practitioner makes. This is not because they are overly passive but because the practitioner is seen as the empowered professional. The practitioner must be able to obtain not only verbal or written agreement from the client, but also to sense when something is "out of synch." This may require intuitive sensitivity to subconscious material and facets of the client that are not fully in conscious awareness.

Resentment usually occurs when a client is put into an awkward situation. Clients frequently test boundaries. The practitioner must consciously decide to keep the integrity of clients' boundaries when clients attempt to significantly relax those boundaries. Because of the power differential, the client's typical response to author- ity figures may dictate the response to the practitioner. In doing so, the client may recreate the same complex elements of similar relationships from the past. Professional helping relationships usu- ally have strong transference elements in which the parent-child relationship is unconsciously re-established. Therefore, it's possible for unresolved needs, feelings and issues from childhood to be transferred to the practitioner. The client may react unconsciously to the practitioner's feelings, thoughts, expectations and beliefs by projecting personal feelings, thoughts, expectations and behaviors onto the practitioner. If this parent-child relationship dynamic manifests, it's essential for the practitioner to be diligent in manag- ing appropriately the power differential in the relationship.

In addition, a practitioner who is not diligent in maintaining the integrity of the power differential may inadvertently disempower a client. Because energy healing methods can result in profound changes, the client may attribute the healing that occurs solely to the skill of the practitioner, not recognizing that ultimately the healer is the client. The client's own inner wisdom and healer may be discounted when the client projects the role onto the practitioner. If the practitioner accepts this projection because of an unconsciousness need to be the "all-knowing healer," it disempowers the client and shifts inappropriately the power differential. A disempowered client may feel victimized by the practitioner and this can lead to claims of unethical behavior by the client against the practitioner and also a potential lawsuit.

To maintain a healthy practice, the empowered practitioner must pay special attention to the needs of the person with less power, the client. It's also essential to ask, how am I encouraging my client to express concerns? How am I obtaining feedback from clients who may not be able to express themselves readily? Am I aware if my client is uncomfortable or becomes disempowered? Not paying close attention to how the power differential is being handled in the therapeutic relationship is considered unethical. It can also lead to legal problems for the practitioner. It's the practitioner's responsibility to honor and maintain the balance of power in the therapeutic relationship in such a way that it does no harm to the client.

Transference in traditional psychology is the process by which emotions and desires originally associated with one person, such as a parent or sibling, are unconsciously shifted to another person, especially to the therapist. For example, the client may begin to feel the same feelings towards the therapist as the client does for a lover. These types of feelings may be positive or negative. When a client personalizes the professional relationship with the practitioner through the process of transference it can diminish the effectiveness of the therapeutic relationship. When a person seeks out a professional caregiver, very key issues of power, trust, and control in the therapeutic relationship become the practitioner's responsibility. The practitioner must be aware of this phenomenon and have the appropriate skills to maintain a professional relationship with the client. Please be aware that the more disorganized, disempowered, and lacking in internal resources clients are, the more susceptible they will be to transferences.

Countertransference is the process by which the practitioner transfers (often unconsciously) the practitioner's emotional needs and feelings toward the client. This can result in the practitioner's personal involvement to the detriment of the therapeutic relationship. For example, the practitioner may seek personal approval from the client or may become irritated with a late client because it reminds the practitioner of her former husband. Or the practitioner can find himself engaging with a client's manipulative tactics because that's how the practitioner relates to his mother. Therefore, countertransference is the inability of the practitioner to separate the therapeutic relationship from the practitioner's personal feelings and expectations of the client. Therefore, practitioners must actively seek ways of preventing excessive client dependency, emphasize personal empowerment as a goal, avoid judgments about a client, seek consultation when experiencing complexities, and refer clients when appropriate.

Dual or multiple relationships in traditional psychology occur when a professional and personal relationship take place simultaneously between the psychologist and the client. According to the American Psychological Association, a psychologist refrains from entering into a dual relationship if the dual relationship could reasonably be expected to impair the psychologist's objectivity, competence, or effectiveness in performing functions as a psychologist, or otherwise risks exploitation or harm to the person with whom the professional relationship exists. Dual relationships can also develop between the practitioner and client within a professional therapeutic relationship if the practitioner is not vigilant in maintaining professional boundaries with clients. For example, this happens when a client asks for the practitioner's home phone number, wants to meet the practitioner for lunch or invites the practitioner to a social event. By taking the relationship outside of the client-practitioner framework, it creates a dual relationship. As a general rule, dual relationships are considered unethical. Mental health care regulations can subject a licensed mental health care professional to professional discipline for engaging in dual relationships which can result in the licensed practitioner losing the license.

As stated above, a core concept of ethics in the helping professions is that the relationship is always client-centered. An ongoing robust *informed consent* process is essential for maintaining a client-centered practice. It is also the cornerstone for building rapport and trust with your clients. Informed consent means the client has a clear understanding of the energy healing method being offered by the practitioner. This means it's incumbent upon the practitioner to be able to explain to the client the theoretical basis of the energy healing method being offered as well as how it is applied or used during a session. In addition, the practitioner should be able to provide information regarding research that has been published and the known efficacy of any energy healing method being offered. How much information a specific client needs will vary. However, all practitioners using energy healing methods should be well prepared to answer client questions in depth and to give credible references for the methods they intend to use.

Another aspect of obtaining informed consent is to give clear information about the *risks and benefits* of any energy healing method used. While the benefits of energy-oriented methods seem to be many, the risks are often not considered as many practitioners are eager to use energy healing methods with clients. However, in truth, there are substantial risks, depending on the client's issues and needs. For example, some energy healing methods can cause physical discomfort or emotional distress that can be perceived as negative. It is also possible for a client to experience in an energy healing session some emotional distress and physical discomfort related to traumatic, upsetting, or stressful experiences encountered earlier in life. Because many energy healing methods can quickly cause a change or transformation, the client could experience cognitive dissonance between the client's beliefs and the new reality. If a client holds the belief that it takes a long time to release trauma, he may be disappointed, even jarred, by a rapid, heretofore unknown freedom from fear and sense of peacefulness. For those who use cognitive-somatic energy practices such as Emotional Freedom Techniques (EFT), it is a well-documented risk that clients generally feel an emotional distance from a traumatic event after applying EFT. This can result in the client being unable to recall specific components of the event. While this is a benefit and a desirable outcome from a therapeutic point of view, it can also be a risk. Emotional distance from a traumatic event can adversely impact the client's ability to provide legal testimony that carries the same emotional impact as prior to applying EFT. So, the risk is that it can be an impediment to the client who needs to go through legal proceedings or an insurance claim that may include a court deposition and providing testimony. Furthermore, a total change in the client's view of the work and self-identity may occur with the rapid mind/body integration that can come with some energy healing methods. Again, this may be desirable for the client but could cause concern for a client living in a family system or culture that requires rigid boundaries and role definitions. A skilled and ethical energy healing practitioner will assist the client in considering these issues. The client must consult his inner wisdom to know if immediate and possibly far-reaching change is a desired outcome for using energy healing methods and is in line with the client's intention and goals.

Informed consent issues with those unable to make independent decisions

THERE ARE TIMES WHEN A practitioner may have an opportunity to use an energy healing method when the primary person (i.e., the intended client) is uninformed or disinterested. This presents vexing ethical dilemmas for the practitioners who are oriented to helping others. Even when practitioners feel they can be of help, there are situations where they may not be able to offer services because of the lack of informed consent from designated guardians. Here are some examples:

- Irritable infants who would benefit from the calming effects of Therapeutic Touch, Healing Touch, or Reiki.
- Hyperactive children who could learn energetic self-management exercises such as Eden Energy Medicine techniques to increase their ability to be calm and focused.
- Teenagers who would benefit from meridian tapping techniques to help them gain self-worth and tools to help calm intense emotions.
- Severely ill people in a hospital or homecare setting with family members present who are skeptical towards energy healing.
- Elderly individuals who would benefit from energy healing methods to help with mental confusion but who have signed over power of attorney for all health care decisions to a designated individual who opposes energy healing methods.
- An unconscious person attended by caregivers who are opposed to energy healing.

The desire of the practitioner to be helpful has to be modified by the realities of each situation. Parents have the right to choose treatment modalities for their children and adolescents until the age of majority is reached. Therefore, practitioners must receive permission and obtain informed consent from the parents or legal guardians of minors in order to use energy healing methods with them. If an elderly person has signed over power of attorney for health care decisions to another person, the practitioner would only be able to offer services with permission and consent of the individual who has the power to make those health care decisions for the elderly person. In the case of severe illness, the practitioner may find it helpful to engage the family in understanding energetic approaches. As a result of this dialogue their resistance may be overcome, especially when the non-invasive nature of energy healing methods bring relief to the patient. Although hospital personnel do not have to be in agreement with using energy healing methods, it is always a good idea to inform them of what the practitioner is doing. When I have done energy healing work in hospitals, most hospital personnel are curious and many support non-traditional complementary and alternative medicine approaches with patients.

Informed consent issues with those who have not directly given it

MANY ENERGY HEALING PRACTITIONERS HAVE developed skills in medical intuition, psychic attunement, surrogate healing, or work with clients at a distance. Clients may seek the services of this type of energy healing practitioner, not for themselves but for a third party. For example, a client may ask the following of the practitioner, "Would you do a reading for my nephew?" "Could you tell me what is going on with my mom?" "Would you do a healing for a friend who has been diagnosed recently with cancer?" If a practitioner agrees to work on an individual without receiving direct informed consent from that individual, the practitioner has taken away the person's autonomy and violated an essential principle of health care ethics. The practitioner has taken away the client's right to make a voluntary, knowing, and informed choice to engage the services of the energy healing practitioner. In addition, the energy healing practitioner has violated the privacy of the person which can lead to a breach of privacy lawsuit. Ethically and legally it is mandatory that the practitioner obtain direct informed consent from the individual being worked on in these situations.

Areas in which ethical violations can occur

IT'S ESSENTIAL FOR ENERGY HEALING practitioners to understand behaviors that are considered unethical by professional codes of ethics. This basis of knowledge assists practitioners to avoid the many problems that can occur in daily practice throughout their careers. Because of the subtleties implied in the practice of energy healing methods, there are many possible areas where misinterpretation by clients and perceived overstepping of boundaries can occur. Below is a list of the most prominent possible ethical violations with examples:

Practicing beyond the scope of practice; exceeding one's skill level

- Doing energy healing methods without appropriate training.
- Working with clients with issues that are beyond the level of training of the practitioner.

Financial impropriety

- Requiring fees from referral professionals.

Failure to honor the fiduciary relationship

- Violating client trust; putting your needs ahead of your client's needs.
- Having a personal agenda.

Inappropriate advertising

- Presenting misleading qualifications or claims in marketing materials.

Violating confidentiality

- Discussing a case with anyone without the permission of the client.
- Name dropping a well-known client at a party.

Bigotry, being judgmental of clients

- Refusing to work with clients because of their race, religion, or sexual orientation.

Misleading claims of curative ability

- Saying to a client that her trauma will be released in a particular number of energy healing sessions.

Sexual misconduct

- Touching a client inappropriately or in a sexual manner.
- Using inappropriate language.

Misrepresentation of education status and skill level

- Representing or identifying yourself as an energy healing practitioner after attending one workshop.

Exploiting the power differential
- Telling a client what to do.
- Asking professional advice from a client (investment, legal, medical, etc.).

Dual relationships
- Exchanging energy healing sessions for house cleaning or other professional services.
- Having a personal relationship with a client.
- Dating a client.
- Inappropriate use of social media such as Facebook friends.

Violation of laws
- Practicing medicine or psychotherapy without a license.
- Failure to comply with your legally defined scope of practice.

Failure to obtain informed consent
- Failure to discuss theoretical basis of the energy healing methods you use with clients.
- Not disclosing that energy healing methods are considered experimental; not disclosing the risks and benefits of the energy healing method(s) you use with clients.
- Using an energy healing method without express permission.
- Touching a client without getting written and verbal permission from the client.

Failure to get adequate consultation
- Not getting the help you need when working with a client who has complex issues.

Ignoring practitioner contraindications
- Working with clients when you are ill or emotionally upset and not able to be fully present and centered with your clients.

Ignoring client contraindications
- Working with clients that are emotionally fragile; that are unable to maintain healthy boundaries; that are not good candidates for energy healing methods.

Practicing below the standard of care

- Using unsubstantiated techniques that are not part of the legally defined scope of practice;
- Using potentially harmful or unsafe therapies with clients.

Failure to refer to another practitioner

- Not referring when a client needs services for which you are not qualified or licensed to provide such as psychological or medical treatment.

Self-accountability as the cornerstone of ethical actions:

IN ESSENCE, SELF-ACCOUNTABILITY IS THE cornerstone of ethics. It is about the decisions you make and who you are when no one's watching you. People who embrace self-accountability are honest with themselves and take responsibility for their speech and actions. When you are self-accountable, you have the ability to look beyond the immediate moment to consider all the consequences of your actions and then be willing to accept them. This personal ethic is the precursor of your professional ethics. You are not likely to be more ethical in your professional life than you are in your personal life.

There is a significant new concept that is emerging: the practitioner and what the practitioner brings to the therapeutic setting as a person is just as important to the outcome of care as the level of skill in the techniques the practitioner uses with client. The nature of the relationship between practitioner and client is at the core of facilitating the healing process. Put another way, who we are as individuals communicates energetically to clients much more than a specific technique or method. Ethical guidelines within a professional group or specialty provide an *external locus of control*. Self-examination of values and motivations stimulates development of *internal locus of control* for those who want to expand their ethical consciousness. External guidelines are helpful, but ultimately you will use your own values and motivations to choose a course of action. Ethical codes are intended to encourage behavior that is more effective therapeutically and discourage behavior that is ineffective or harmful.

Boundaries

IN RELATIONSHIPS, A BOUNDARY IS a limit that separates one person from another. It protects the integrity of each person. A boundary can be as tangible as the skin that surrounds our body or as intangible as each person's energy field. Understanding boundaries is crucial to creating an ethical practice and building professional relationships. The practitioner who increases awareness of the client's boundaries, what the client is comfortable with and what the client is not comfortable with, as well as the practitioner's own boundaries, can improve the therapeutic relationship. This helps practitioners avoid many inadvertent slips into unethical behavior. Boundary issues between a practitioner and a client are especially sensitive. When a client permits the practitioner to touch, the client is in a vulnerable state, which can be stressful. This state of vulnerability often places the client in uncharted territory. The client may not be aware of personal needs, options, or what constitutes appropriate boundaries and behavior. Because of this ambiguity, the practitioner needs to be aware of and sensitive to the boundary issues of the client.

It's not uncommon for clients to push boundaries. For example, some clients tend to put the practitioner on a pedestal, which can be detrimental to the therapeutic relationship. Also, most practitioners will at some time encounter the "needy" client. This type of client can show up in many ways, such as wanting excessive contact with the practitioner. These needy clients may send many emails or make numerous phone calls seeking reassurances or problem solving from the practitioner instead of dealing with the issues in a session. Some clients may ask to meet the practitioner for coffee or some other social engagement, which pushes the boundary into a dual relationship situation that in most cases is wise to avoid.

There are at least five major types of interpersonal boundaries: physical, emotional, intellectual, energetic, and sexual.

- **Physical** – The physical boundary is the physical space contained with the invisible line present in all human interactions. It may expand or shrink depending on the individual's level of comfort and safety. Most of us are aware of when our physical boundary is crossed. We do not want strangers to get too close but a good friend doesn't create the same boundary concerns. How much personal space we need depends on the circumstances. Physical boundaries also vary in a professional setting. Physical boundaries can shift depending on whether touch is involved in the therapeutic process.

- **Emotional** – Emotions are major aspects of our personal identity. The emotional boundary is also variable, depending on the situation, and it influences whether or not a person expresses his feelings. It's essential for practitioners to be aware of their own emotional boundaries and those of their clients.'

- **Intellectual** – The intellectual boundary encompasses a person's belief system, their worldview, values, opinions, and thoughts. In an ethical practice, it's imperative for the practitioner to be fully present in a space of compassionate detachment for his or her clients. A judgmental practitioner is not serving the client nor conducting his or her practice in the most ethical manner.

- **Energetic** – According to many theories of energy healing, all humans have a constant flow of energy that permeates and surrounds them. The energy patterns of one person can influence those of another. We are energetic beings who need to maintain our energetic boundaries as well as our physical, emotional, mental, and sexual boundaries. Practitioners of energy-based modalities are trained to work with the energy systems of their clients. A skilled energy healing practitioner stays centered to protect his or her own energy from the influence of the client's energetic disturbances and does not allow his or her own energy to inappropriately cross the client's energetic boundary.

- **Sexual** – Health care professionals should not have sexual relationships with their clients. Violating the sexual boundaries of a client can violate all the other boundaries as well. Respecting the sexual boundary is not only the ethical choice; it's also the healing choice.

> These boundaries can be compromised by either party but remember it's the practitioner's responsibility to manage the boundaries within a therapeutic relationship.

Practitioner vulnerabilities, which can lead to unethical behavior

IT IS THE NATURE OF being human to be vulnerable in some areas of our lives. Personal fears and spiritual longings correlate with the vulnerabilities each person carries. As a consequence, the therapeutic relationship contains the vulnerabilities of both the practitioner and the client. The more conscious the practitioner is of personal vulnerabilities, the more effective the practitioner can be in not bringing those issues into the healing relationship.

Unmanageable levels of personal vulnerability by a practitioner can lead to unethical behavior. Issues that can directly affect the therapeutic relationship and cause ethical violations are fear of intimacy, crises in personal relationships, feelings of failure, low self-esteem, poor impulse control, professional isolation, and depression (Cohen 2003). In addition, longing to be the perfect healer, desiring to control the therapeutic relationship, and holding onto a needy client for financial security can also create ethical issues in one's practice.

Vulnerabilities to unethical behavior can be found in the following areas:

- Practitioner's disregard for the client.
- Practitioner burnout.
- Practitioner's ignorance of the pitfalls.

- Underestimation of the power of the energetic exchange to affect the practitioner.
- Practitioner's own unexamined personal issues.
- Practitioner's unacknowledged longing for love and spiritual connection.
- Practitioner's failure to refer when appropriate (Taylor, 1995.)

In additional to the list above, as provided in Kylea Taylor's book *The Ethics of Caring*, other vulnerabilities may include:

- Unhealthy desire to save or rescue people.
- Imposing or projecting personal issues on to the client.
- Failure to consider individual gender and cultural differences of the client.
- Failure to refer when the client's needs fall outside the legally defined scope of practice of the practitioner.
- Failure to refer even if the practitioner can legally work with the client, if the practitioner is not competent and skilled in meeting the client's needs.

> It is critical to know that ethical violations can lead to legal liability.

As provided under the previous section on "Self-accountability", when you have a well-developed sense of self-accountability, you are honest with yourself, and you are fully responsible for what you say and do. As an energy healing practitioner, you are only as good to the extent to where your own healing work has taken you. Self-accountability will be a key ally for how you deal with your own vulnerability as an energy healing practitioner.

Core values assessment exercise

A SATISFYING AND BALANCED LIFE occurs when your values are congruent with the way you lead your life and conduct your energy healing practice. After all, they are the major conscious and unconscious influences on the decisions you make through-out your personal life and your professional career as a healing arts practitioner.

Taking the time to go deeply into the following questions helps clarify your core values and assists you in formulating your own personal honor code for the practice of energy healing methods. External guidelines are helpful but ultimately you will use your own values and motivations to choose a course of action. That's why examining your core values and having a personal honor code are essential for practicing energy healing methods.

> Please give these questions some deep thought as they can expand and enhance your ethical consciousness and help you create your own personal honor code.

- What are my attitudes and beliefs about wellness?
- What are the most important *personal* characteristics for me as an energy healing practitioner?
- What are the key *professional* characteristics for me as an energy healing practitioner?
- How do my values affect my work with clients and enhance professionalism?

Section III

Key Legal Principles for Energy Healing Practitioners

THE PURPOSE OF THIS SECTION is to provide you with the opportunity to gain an understanding about the essential legal principles that apply to both licensed and non-licensed energy healing practitioners. Also, in this section you will learn about health care freedom laws and risk management strategies you can implement to help protect your practice.

> It's critical to remember your scope of practice as an energy healing practitioner is ultimately defined by law.

Licensure and scope of practice

AS STATED IN THE INTRODUCTION, energy healing practitioners are either licensed health care providers or non-licensed providers depending on the laws and regulations in the state in which they practice. While both groups are subject to legal liabilities, each group has separate issues to consider.

Physicians are licensed in all fifty states and they must comply with the laws and regulations that govern the practice of medicine. By using an innovative energy healing method with patients, a physician may be subject to professional discipline and a malpractice claim. This is because energy healing methods are not currently recognized as part of a physician's legally defined scope of practice. Also, practicing innovative and unsubstantiated energy healing methods can be legally determined to be per se malpractice. For example, if a physician used an energy healing method such as Matrix Energetics with patients, a medical board could take the position that the practice of Matrix Energetics falls below the standards of practice or outside the acceptable scope of practice of medicine. Therefore, if the physician used Matrix Energetics with patients it could be considered unprofessional conduct and lead to probation, suspension, or revocation of the physician's medical license. It could also lead to a malpractice claim from a patient.

There have been several disciplinary cases brought against physicians for using energy healing methods with patients because the medical boards considered those methods to be "unsubstantiated therapy." Some physicians have even lost their licenses to practice medicine because of using energy healing methods with patients. However, others have been able to retain their licenses after a long expensive court battle. It's important to recognize that disciplinary cases are not generally brought against a physician solely because an unsubstantiated energy healing method was used with patients. These kinds of cases always involve the specific facts and details of how the energy healing method is being used by the physician with patients. Two physicians could incorporate the same energy healing method into their respective practices with one never having any difficulty and the other being disciplined. One may practice good medicine and use the energy healing method to complement standard medical treatment while the other does not.

Some states, such as Oregon, have a law that protects physicians from professional discipline for using a CAM method as long as the patient signs an informed consent agreement for the CAM method offered by the physician. Also, the CAM method cannot take the place of traditional medical practices and it must not cause harm to the patient. In addition, the physician must demonstrate training and competency in the CAM method used and there must be one other physician in the state of Oregon who uses the same CAM method. Laws vary by state, and medical boards can be tough on physicians who practice in a way that is not recognizable according to the prevailing consensus medical standards of care.

To reduce the risk of professional discipline, one of the best risk management strategies for a physician, who uses an energy healing method, is to demonstrate to the board that the physician is competently trained in the energy healing method. This is best demonstrated by being certified by a professional training organization in the energy healing method. Another essential risk management tool is to have a legally sound Informed Consent/Agreement for CAM Services that patients sign. To provide maximum protection this agreement needs to be customized and drafted specifically for the physician's practice.

Psychologists and other **licensed mental health professionals** are also licensed in all fifty states and they must comply with the laws and regulations that govern the practice of psychotherapy. Like physicians, by using an innovative energy healing method with patients, a licensed mental health care professional may be subject to professional discipline and malpractice claim. This is because energy healing methods are not currently recognized as part of their legally defined scope of practice. Also, just as with physicians, it can be legally determined to be per se malpractice for licensed mental health care professionals to use energy healing methods with patients. For example, if a psychologist used an energy healing method such as Reiki with patients, a psychology board could take the position that the practice of Reiki falls below the standards of practice or outside the acceptable scope of practice of psychology. Therefore, if the psychologist used Reiki with patients, it could be considered unprofessional conduct and could lead to probation, suspension, or revocation of the psychologist's license. It could also lead to a malpractice claim from the patient.

There have been several disciplinary cases brought against licensed mental health care professionals for using energy healing methods because the boards considered those methods to be "unsubstantiated therapy." In one case, a psychologist was ordered to cease using EFT in his psychotherapy practice. If he wanted to use EFT with clients, he had to create a coaching practice, completely separate from his psychotherapy practice. In another case, a licensed clinical social worker was using an energy healing method to remove "entities" from patients. She lost her license.

To reduce the risk of professional discipline, one of the best risk management strategies for a psychotherapist, who uses an energy healing method, is to demonstrate to the board that the psychotherapist is competently trained in the energy healing method. This is best demonstrated by being certified by a professional training organization in the energy healing method. For example, if a licensed professional counselor used EFT in his practice, then it would be an excellent risk management strategy for that licensed professional counselor to be certified in EFT by an organization that is a member of the National Alliance of Energy Practitioners. Also, another good risk management strategy would be for the licensed professional counselor to consider becoming a member of the Association for Comprehensive Energy Psychology (ACEP). ACEP, as a professional organization, brings credibility to EFT as a viable psychotherapy intervention. This is because ACEP has a large member base, standards of care, an ethics code, and conducts research on energy psychology methods such as EFT. Another essential risk management tool is to have a legally sound Informed Consent/Agreement for Psychotherapy Services that patients sign. To provide maximum protection this agreement needs to be customized and drafted specifically for the psychotherapist's practice.

Licensed allied health care professionals can be subject to professional discipline, a malpractice claim and being charged with practicing a profession without a license. For example, if a physical therapist uses the Emotion Code to help patients not only with pain management but also the underlying emotional trauma, it could be perceived that the physical therapist is practicing psychotherapy without a license. While treating physical pain is part of a physical therapist's legally defined scope of practice, treating emotional trauma is not. In addition, if the physical therapist uses the Emotion Code with patients, her licensing board could take the position that the practice of the Emotion Code falls below the standards of care or outside the acceptable scope of practice of physical therapy. Therefore, if the physical therapist used the Emotion Code with patients, it could be considered unprofessional conduct and could lead to probation, suspension, or revocation of the physical therapist's license. It could also lead to a malpractice claim from the patient.

Like with other licensed health care professionals, to reduce the risk of professional discipline, one of the best risk management strategies for a physical therapist, who uses an energy healing method, is to demonstrate to the board that the he is competently trained in the energy healing method. For our example above, this is best demonstrated by being certified in the Emotion Code.

Based on the above discussion, the two most significant legal risks licensed practitioners face in using energy healing methods with patients is a malpractice claim and being subject to a professional discipline.

Non-licensed energy healing practitioners are subject to negligence claims but are not subject to professional discipline by a licensing board. However, non-licensed energy healing practitioners are exposed to being charged with the crime of practicing a profession without a license. Consequently, while a practitioner is competently practicing a specific energy healing method as it was taught, the practitioner could still be in violation of the law. For example, a non-licensed EFT practitioner may be very skilled but still could not work with a client suffering from anxiety. Because anxiety is a psychological disorder, the EFT practitioner could be charged for the unlawful practice of psychotherapy. Even in those states that have enacted health care freedom legislation, which can protect non-licensed practitioners from being charged with practicing a licensed profession, they still must tread carefully in how they conduct their practices.

> Non-licensed energy healing practitioners could mistakenly believe they are safe from prosecution because they are practicing within their scope of practice as it was taught to them either through a certification program or other type of training.

It's imperative for non-licensed practitioners to be aware of the Diagnostic and Statistical Manual for Mental Disorders, Edition 5 (DSM-5) because it defines all the major categories of mental illness. As a general rule only licensed mental health care professionals can consult, evaluate, treat, and/or diagnose psychological disorders listed in the DSM-5. There are a few exceptions like the state of Colorado, which allows non-licensed practitioners to practice psychotherapy provided they register and comply with the regulations promulgated by the Colorado Department of Regulatory Agencies. Therefore, it's important to know the laws in your state.

Based on the foregoing, non-licensed energy healing practitioners are safe to work with clients for stress management. However, they should not work with clients who have psychological disorders such as abuse, trauma, anxiety, PTSD, phobias, depression, etc. This is because these are all considered psychological disorders as listed in the DSM-5. This is true even if the non-licensed practitioner has a background in mental health, including a masters or PhD in psychology or counseling. *Having a degree of any kind is not a license to practice!* If a client is suffering from a psychological disorder such as PTSD, then the non-licensed practitioner needs to refer that client to a licensed mental health care professional who is competent in treating PTSD. If the non-licensed practitioner fails to refer the client to the appropriate licensed provider, it can result in harm to the client. This failure to refer subjects the practitioner to a negligence claim from the client and being charged with the crime of practicing psychotherapy without a license.

Based on the above discussion, the two most significant legal risks non-licensed practitioners face in using energy healing methods with clients is a negligence claim and being charged with practicing a licensed profession without a license.

Scenarios to consider regarding licensure and scope of practice issues

In exploring the scenarios below, I will discuss general legal principles that apply in most states. However, there are exceptions depending on the particular laws and regulations of the state in which the energy healing practitioner practices. The discussion is based on the perception that a licensing board, regulatory agency or court of law would most likely have in regards to the scenario. Thus, the scenario is being viewed through the lens of the current legal and regulatory system that governs healing arts practitioners.

Scenario #1

SALLY IS A NON-LICENSED REIKI practitioner offering her services as a stress management consultant. Tom contacts her to help him feel less stress and more confident at public speaking because he will be soon presenting at a major conference. In the first session, Tom tells Sally that his father tended to cut him off when he wanted to say something at the dinner table. That made him feel self-conscious. He thinks this may be why he has a fear of public speaking.

In their third session, Tom reveals that not only did his father cut him off at the dinner table but would also verbally berate him. His father would tell him that he would amount to nothing which Tom now realizes damaged his self-esteem.

During their fifth Reiki session, Tom tells Sally that memories are surfacing between appointments where he is remembering that his father was not only verbally abusive but would also slap him if he spoke up. Tom tells Sally he feels physically sick to his stomach, anxious, and depressed thinking about what his father did to him as a child.

Discussion - One of the issues to consider in the above scenario is whether Sally violated any licensure laws at any time in her sessions with Tom. In other words, was Sally practicing psychotherapy without a license?

In the beginning it would most likely be the perception that Sally was not practicing psychotherapy without a license. Helping Tom feel less stress and more confident in public speaking is not considered to be psychotherapy. However, what began to surface during the third session should have alerted Sally that Tom endured verbal abuse from his father. This could indicate that deeper psychological issues may be present rather than Tom just being stressed about public speaking. This is a gray area where it could possibly be perceived that Sally had crossed the line from stress management consulting to practicing psychotherapy. If Sally is an experienced Reiki practitioner with a background in psychology or mental health, then the shade of gray would be light. If Sally does not have a background in psychology or mental health, then the shade of gray would be dark.

During the fifth session, memories surface that Tom had suffered physical abuse from his father, and he clearly exhibited psychological symptoms. If Sally continued to work with Tom, under most psychotherapy practice acts, she would be considered practicing psychotherapy without a license. This would be true regardless of whether Sally felt it was within her scope of practice as a Reiki practitioner to continue working with Tom or if Tom wanted to continue working with her. At this point, the ethical and client-centered choice for Sally is to refer Tom to a licensed mental health counselor to assist Tom in dealing with his psychological symptoms.

Scenario #2

STEVE IS A REAL ESTATE broker who likes energy healing for relaxation and to relieve his day-to-day stress. His massage therapist, Mark, blends energy balancing techniques with somatic work. They have established a good working partnership. During a session, when Steve is in a deeply relaxed state, he starts to remember childhood trauma of witnessing his father beat his mother. After the session, Mark knows something is amiss but Steve isn't willing to talk about it. Mark feels he was doing good work but also knows that deep relaxation can lead to a client reliving traumatic biographical events. Steve cancels the next appointment to avoid further pain. What is the best course of action for Mark to take regarding Steve?

> **Discussion** - Mark could let Steve drift away as a client. However, it would be best if Mark enlisted the help of a licensed mental health counselor. The counselor can offer assistance to Steve to unearth the painful memories in a way that can allow healing to begin. While under the care of the counselor, Steve can continue to receive the benefits of the energy work and massages. However, if Mark continues to work with Steve without the counselor to help him heal his painful memories, it is possible Mark could be accused of practicing psychotherapy without a license.

Scenario #3

DAN IS A NON-LICENSED MERIDIAN tapping practitioner offering his services as a peak performance coach specializing in sports performance. In interviewing a potential new client, Jessica, who is a nationally ranked college tennis player, Jessica tells Dan that she is currently taking anti-depressant medication prescribed by her psychologist. She is also prone to angry emotional outbursts on the court if she is losing a match. She wants Tom to help her stop this behavior and to be more positive and focused during matches. Dan agrees to work with her and after several sessions Jessica tells Dan that she is playing better matches and her outlook is more positive. She tells Tom that wants to stop taking her anti-depressants.

Discussion - One of the main issues to consider in the above scenario is whether Dan should have accepted Jessica as a client when she disclosed in her initial conversation that she was on anti-depressant medication and was in the care of a psychologist. Again, this is a gray area because Jessica is receiving psychological care at the same time she wants to engage Dan as a peak performance coach.

If Dan has a robust informed consent process with Jessica that includes 1) gaining an understanding of Jessica's psychological situation, including consulting with Jessica's psychologist for integrated care and; 2) having Jessica sign a legally sound Client Agreement which clearly discloses that Dan is not a licensed psychotherapist and solely offers his services as a peak performance coach, then that may reduce his legal vulnerability of being perceived as practicing psychotherapy without a license.

This type of robust informed consent process is an excellent risk management strategy for Dan to implement This is the case not only with Jessica but for every client he works with in his meridian tapping practice. In addition to having a robust informed consent process with Jessica, it's equally critical that Dan only provide meridian tapping that focuses on Jessica's performance as a tennis player and not on her psychological disorders. If Dan focuses on Jessica's psychological disorders, it could be perceived that he is practicing psychotherapy without a license. However, if Dan is working in conjunction with Jessica's psychologist, then as an integrated approach it may be possible for Dan to apply meridian tapping to the events Jessica's psychologist has treated to help release any remaining energetic impact to those events. Again, this is a gray area, and Dan would need to tread very carefully in order to not be perceived as practicing psychotherapy without a license.

The second issue to discuss is how Dan should handle the situation when Jessica tells him she wants to stop taking her medication. She feels that she doesn't need it anymore after working with him. Here the answer is in black and white. No, Dan cannot advise Jessica to stop taking her medications. Only Jessica's psychologist who prescribed the medication can advise Jessica about stopping her medication.

Scenario #4

MARY IS A LICENSED PROFESSIONAL counselor who took a level one Matrix Energetics weekend seminar. Mary is excited about what she learned at the seminar and immediately begins identifying and advertising herself as a Matrix Energetics practitioner. The following week she tells her relatively new patient, James, she wants to use Matrix Energetics as part of his psychotherapy session. He feels skeptical but because Mary has told him she is a Matrix Energetics practitioner and she's so enthusiastic about using Matrix Energetics that he reluctantly agrees to use it in his session. James cancels his next session and tells Mary he no longer wants to be her patient.

Discussion – One issue in the above scenario is whether or not Mary's conduct with James makes her vulnerable to being subject to professional discipline. Yes, first Mary identified and represented herself as a Matrix Energetics practitioner and used Matrix Energetics with a patient after only taking a level one Matrix Energetics seminar. Her licensing board would take the position that a weekend workshop does not make her competent to use Matrix Energetics as a therapy with patients. Second, her licensing board would likely take the position that Mary was practicing below the standards of care and outside of her legally defined scope of practice as a licensed professional counselor in using Matrix Energetics. Third, the licensing board would take the position that Mary engaged in unprofessional conduct, as it could easily be perceived that Mary misrepresented her credentials and coerced James into trying Matrix Energetics.

Another issue is that Mary has also made herself vulnerable to a malpractice lawsuit if James decides to pursue legal action against her. Three of the legal principles James could assert in his malpractice claim is that Mary used an unsubstantiated method, misrepresented her credentials, and failed to obtain informed consent from James.

Scenario #4A

WHAT IF MARY WAS ENROLLED in the Matrix Energetics certification program and needed to begin using Matrix Energetics with patients in order to become certified?

Discussion – There is a fine distinction between claiming to be a Matrix Energetics practitioner and using Matrix Energetics with patients after taking a level one seminar and being enrolled in the Matrix Energetics certification program. If Mary does not represent herself as a Matrix Energetics practitioner and fully discloses to her patients these specifics: 1) that she has taken a level one Matrix Energetics seminar; 2) is enrolled in the Matrix Energetics certification program, and needs practice sessions for certification; 3) that she has each patient agree to using Matrix Energetics in the session; 4) that she has each patient sign a Permission Agreement consenting to being a practice client, she may be able to defend herself against a claim from her licensing board for practicing below her standards of care. She would also be less likely to expose herself to a malpractice claim from a patient who felt pressured into trying Matrix Energetics.

Scenario #5

CHERYL IS A REGISTERED NURSE who is also a trained in Therapeutic Touch. The hospital has granted approval for her to use Therapeutic Touch with patients. Cheryl uses Therapeutic Touch, with permission from the patients, as a way to help them release the stress and anxiousness they feel regarding upcoming surgical procedures. After a year, Cheryl gets a new nursing assignment to work with patients suffering from diabetes, a chronic condition. After using Therapeutic Touch with Veronica for several weeks, Veronica unlocks a memory she had buried for many years that she was sexually abused as a child. Cheryl continues to see Veronica as a diabetic patient in the hospital but shifts her focus from dealing with her chronic diabetes to using Therapeutic Touch to treat Veronica's underlying emotional distress about the sexual abuse trauma she suffered as a child. Cheryl believes that treating the underlying sexual abuse trauma with Therapeutic Touch will assist Veronica in managing her diabetes.

Discussion – The issue to consider in the above scenario is if Cheryl violated any licensure laws at any time in her Therapeutic Touch sessions with Veronica. In other words, did she cross the line from practicing nursing to practicing psychotherapy?

It would most likely be the perception that Cheryl was not practicing psychotherapy without a license by using Therapeutic Touch to help patients feel less stress and anxious about their surgical procedures or with a chronic medical condition such as diabetes. By using Therapeutic Touch in this manner, it would most likely be considered part of her scope of practice as a nurse.

However, it is possible that Cheryl could be perceived as practicing psychotherapy without a license when she continued to use Therapeutic Touch to treat Veronica's underlying emotional distress about the sexual abuse trauma she suffered as a child. At this point, the ethical and client-centered choice for Cheryl is to refer Veronica to a licensed mental health counselor who can assist Veronica in dealing with the emotional trauma of her history of sexual abuse.

What if Cheryl decides to quit her job at the hospital and open a wellness clinic offering Therapeutic Touch sessions? That would be fine provided Cheryl did not violate any licensure laws. For example, she could offer wellness services using Therapeutic Touch in the same manner as she did in the hospital under her nursing license. However, if Cheryl used Therapeutic Touch to work with patients around traumatic emotional events, then it's possible she would be perceived to be practicing psychotherapy without a license. This would be the case even if the patient did not have an official diagnosis of a DSM-5 disorder. The more traumatic and emotionally impactful the events are, the more likely a licensing board will take the position that using Therapeutic Touch to treat such emotional issues is the practice of psychotherapy. The exception would be if Cheryl was licensed as a psychiatric nurse which under her licensure allows her to treat patients with psychological issues. This is a very gray area. So it's critical for energy healing practitioners who are not licensed mental health care professionals to tread carefully in using energy healing methods to clear significant traumatic emotional events.

Scenario #6

JANET IS A WELLNESS COACH and a certified Healing Touch practitioner but she is not a licensed health care provider. Stacy engages Janet to help her because she suffers from joint pain and severe exhaustion. How should Janet proceed with Stacy?

> **Discussion** – Because joint pain and severe exhaustion can indicate a serious medical condition, Janet should only work with Stacy as a wellness coach and Healing Touch practitioner in conjunction with her medical provider. If Janet renders services to Stacy without Stacy receiving medical diagnosis and treatment, Janet could be considered practicing medicine without a license. If Stacy's conditions worsen under Janet's solo care, then in addition to being charged with practicing medicine without a license, Stacy could sue Janet for negligence.

Health care freedom legislation

There are a number of states that have passed health care freedom legislation. This legislation   is intended to allow non-licensed alternative healing arts practitioners to offer their services to the public without the threat of being charged with practicing medicine. These are called "safe harbor" laws and they are based on the essential health care ethical principle of autonomy. These laws are being driven by consumers who want the freedom to choose their practitioners and to use CAM methods. In order for an alternative healing arts practitioner to be covered by the law, they must comply with the requirements of the law. Generally, this means the practitioner must refrain from certain activities such as conducting surgery, diagnosing, or recommending the client discontinue prescribed medication(s). In addition, some states require that certain disclosures must be made, and a specifically worded Client Agreement and Disclosure Statement must be signed and kept for a number of years. Currently, California, New Mexico, Minnesota, Nevada and Colorado have the most detailed and robust legislation. Other states that have health care freedom laws are Idaho, Rhode Island, Louisiana, and Oklahoma. While all of these state's health care freedom laws are designed to protect non-licensed practitioners from being charged with the unlawful practice of medicine, New Mexico's law is broader. It protects non-licensed practitioner from any licensing law relating to health care services. So, while the other states only protect non-licensed practitioners from the threat of being charged with practicing medicine without a license, New Mexico's law includes mental health care services and even veterinarian services.

These laws can provide non-licensed practitioners more freedom in offering their energy healing services to the public. However, it has been my experience that a vast majority of non-licensed practitioners residing in a state with a health care freedom law are completely unaware of it. Also, even if non-licensed practitioners are aware that their state has a health care freedom law, the practitioners are not following the requirements of the law. This results in non-licensed practitioners not being protected by the law. It leaves them vulnerable to being charged with the unlawful practice of medicine. Full compliance with the requirements of the law is the only way non-licensed practitioners can protect themselves.

Advocates of health care freedom legislation have formed individual state health care freedom organizations for the purpose of lobbying for CAM legislation. These organizations seek to allow alternative healing arts practitioners to offer their services to the public. Also, their purpose is to ensure citizens have access to alternative healing arts practitioners and to use the legal process to protect health care choices. For more information please visit www.nationalhealthfreedom.org.

Working with clients across state lines; using electronic platforms

Because energy healing methods can be applied non-locally and at a distance, many energy healing practitioners work with clients outside of the state where they have their practice. Under current laws, for example, if a non-licensed energy healing practitioner resides in California and works with clients in Illinois using an electronic platform such as Zoom, then the energy healing practitioner is not only subject to the laws and regulations of California but also the laws and regulations of Illinois. So, while in California the energy healing practitioner has the benefit the California's health care freedom law, the practitioner does not have the benefit of California's "safe harbor" law in Illinois. Therefore, it can increase the legal liability for energy healing practitioners to offer their services across state lines.

All licensed health care professionals can only work directly with patients in the state in which they are licensed. Some states allow out-of-state licensed practitioners to render limited services to patients in that state. However, in general, in order to treat patients, the provider must be licensed in the state in which the patient resides. Consequently, licensed health care professionals using an energy healing method with patients may be charged with practicing without a license if they work with individuals outside of the state in which they are licensed. One option licensed health care professionals may consider, if they want to use energy healing methods with clients in other states, is to have a separate coaching or energy healing practice. A number of risk management strategies would need to be implemented to reduce the risks in creating such a separate practice. These include having a separate website and bank accounts between the practitioner's licensed practice and coaching or energy healing practice. In addition, the practitioner would need to have a Client Agreement that expressly disclosed that the practitioner was solely offering energy healing or coaching services and not licensed health care services.

Working with practice clients while enrolled in a certification program

As part of an energy healing certification program, trainees generally must obtain direct clinical experience using the energy healing method with practice clients. During this phase of a certification program, trainees will need to behave ethically and follow the guidelines above regarding offering practice sessions within their legally defined scope of practice. Just because they are in a certification program and may not have established an official practice, trainees are still subject to the laws and regulations that govern helping professionals. This is true even if the trainee does not charge for an energy healing practice session. Many certification programs require trainees to write documentation such as case studies and submit them to the organization for review. Some certification programs also require the trainee to record or film a practice session and submit it to the organization for evaluation. The main purpose for case studies and recorded practice sessions is so that the organization can assess the competency of the trainee. This assessment is part of process to determine if the trainee has met the criteria to become a certified practitioner. It's critical for the trainee to receive written permission in the form of a Permission Agreement (informed consent) from each practice client. In this Permission Agreement the practice client agrees 1) to participate in the practice session with the trainee for the purpose of the trainee's certification requirements; 2) to allow the trainee to document and or record the practice session; and 3) grant permission for the trainee to have the documentation or recording evaluated by the organization. Without the Permission Agreement, the trainee and the organization face potential legal liability from the practice client for failure to obtain informed consent, breach of confidentiality, and invasion of privacy.

There is a distinction between wanting to become a skilled energy healing practitioner (certified or otherwise) and representing and advertising yourself as an energy healing practitioner after taking a weekend workshop, reading a book, or reviewing a tutorial on the Internet. As a general rule, it is considered highly unethical to take a weekend workshop, read a book, or study a tutorial on the Internet for an energy healing technique and then immediately represent and advertise yourself as a practitioner of that energy healing technique. The perception is that no one can become skilled and proficient using an energy healing technique after such limited learning experiences. Skill and proficiency in an energy healing technique comes with further training, practicing, and mentoring.

The myth of internet ordination

I quite often get asked if getting ordained over the Internet protects a non-licensed practitioner from being prosecuted for practicing a licensed profession without a license. The answer is NO! Paying a nominal sum and filling out a form to become an ordained minister may allow, for example, the individual to perform a marriage ceremony in California. However, it does not grant the individual the right to perform healing services. This myth may have gotten started because most psychology practice acts do not apply to qualified members of the clergy who provide pastoral or spiritual counseling to parishioners. However, buying a form on the Internet that says you are an ordained minister does not make you a qualified member of the clergy. It does not protect you from being charged with practicing psychology without a license. Here is a portion of the Psychology Practice Act for the State of Texas, which provides the law does not apply to a recognized member of the clergy:

Sec. 501.004. APPLICABILITY (a) This chapter does not apply to:
4) the activity or service of a recognized member of the clergy who is acting within the person's ministerial capabilities if the person does not:
(A) represent that the person is a psychologist; or
(B) describe the service provided by using the term "psychological";

A licensing board or court of law would interpret this law to mean the following:

- That the practitioner has a degree in theology or other legitimate credentials.
- That the practitioner is a recognized member of the clergy.
- That the practitioner is providing services that would be defined as ministerial.

Consequently, a licensing board or court of law would not recognize being ordained over the Internet as meeting the requirements of the law. Therefore, it would not exempt the practitioner from being charged with practicing psychology without a license.

Do you need a license to touch for energy healing methods?

Another question that often comes up in consultations with my clients or during one of my presentations is "do I need a license to touch?" The answer is not necessarily and it depends. The real question is, is the "touch" you are using with a client considered the practice of a licensed profession? There are a number of energy healing methods where practitioners touch clients. These include methods such as Healing Touch, Reiki, Therapeutic Touch, and Eden Energy Medicine. Some energy healing methods such as EFT or other tapping techniques are generally self-administered by the client. However, there are circumstances when during a tapping session, the practitioner may tap directly on a client. Also, some energy healing practitioners incorporate applied kinesiology or "muscle testing" as part of their practice.

I think it's reasonable to argue that using the touch of a human hand as a tool for moving and harmonizing the body's energies and fields, "tapping" on a client, or using applied kinesiology would not be considered the practice of a licensed profession such as medicine, nursing, or psychotherapy – provided the practitioner was not diagnosing or treating medical conditions or mental health disorders. However, in some states using human touch in this way is considered the practice of massage. Consequently, in those states the practitioner would need to be a licensed massage therapist in order to perform energy healing methods with clients. What's imperative is that the energy healing practitioner receives both verbal and written permission from the client to use any kind of touch. Written permission to touch should be included in the practitioner's Client Agreement & Disclosure Statement.

How do you know if your state requires you to be a licensed massage therapist in order to offer energy healing methods to the public? The first step is to conduct research or seek professional advice to determine if your state regulates the practice of massage. Most states do require licensure to practice massage but a few states do not. If your state does regulate the practice of massage, the second step is to understand the law and how it defines the "practice of massage". The third step is to determine if there is an exception to the law for hands-on energy healing methods. Most states have a broad legal definition of the practice of massage that does not specifically address the use of energy healing methods. This type of definition generally means that the licensing board has broad discretionary powers. Just because a massage practice act does not include hands-on energy healing methods in the definition of the practice of massage does not necessarily mean that you do not need to be a licensed massage therapist in order to practice hands-on energy healing methods. As an example, below is Nebraska's law that defines the practice of massage:

Massage Therapy Practice Act Nebraska

38-1706. Massage therapy defined. Massage therapy means the physical, mechanical, or electrical manipulation of soft tissue for the therapeutic purposes of enhancing muscle relaxation, reducing stress, improving circulation, or instilling a greater sense of well-being and may include the use of oil, salt glows, heat lamps, and hydrotherapy. Massage therapy does not include diagnosis or treatment or use of procedures for which a license to practice medicine or surgery, chiropractic, or podiatry is required nor the use of microwave diathermy, shortwave diathermy, ultrasound, transcutaneous electric nerve stimulation, electrical stimulation of thirty-five volts, neurological hyperstimulation, or spinal and joint adjustments.

In reading the law, you might reasonably conclude that hands-on energy healing methods do not meet the criteria to be considered the practice of massage in Nebraska. Therefore, you do not need to a licensed massage therapist in order to offer hands-on energy healing methods. However, in a blog article published in 2016 by Eric Boehm, the Nebraska Massage Therapy Board took a different position with a Reiki practitioner. I would argue that even though Reiki involves touch, it does not resemble massage therapy in any other way. For example, clients remain fully clothed throughout the session and there is no physical manipulation of soft tissue. Nevertheless, the Board sent a cease and desist letter to the Reiki practitioner for practicing massage without a license. Unfortunately, as a result she was forced to close her Reiki practice. The Reiki practitioner could have hired an attorney to argue that Reiki is not the practice of massage. Therefore, she does not need to be licensed to have a Reiki practice. She may have prevailed but due to the high costs of defending her case, she did not have the financial resources to hire an attorney and argue her case before the Board.

Tennessee like Nebraska does not include hands-on energy healing methods in its massage practice act. However, it does have a policy statement regarding hands-on energy healing methods. Below is Tennessee's policy statement which basically states that if you touch a client doing "energy work", you must be a licensed massage therapist.

Tennessee Massage Licensure Board Policy re: Reiki and Energy Work

Massage is defined by statute as "manipulation of the soft tissues of the client with the intention of positively affecting the health and well-being of the client". T.C.A. Section 63-18-102(3). Any person practicing massage for compensation must be licensed by the Tennessee Massage Licensure Board unless otherwise exempt. T.C.A. Section 63-18-104. The Board has been asked whether Reiki or other "energy work" (including but limited to "healing touch therapy", "quantum touch therapy", etc.) constitutes the practice of massage in Tennessee. It is the Board's opinion that any technique that does not include any touch of the body does not meet the definition of massage in Tennessee. However, the Board is aware that Reiki and other "energy work" often involves the practitioner touching the client's body and manipulating the client's soft issues through various techniques. It is the Board's opinion that any technique that does include such soft tissue manipulation constitutes the practice of massage in Tennessee, and the practitioner should therefore by licensed by the Board unless otherwise exempt pursuant to T.C.A. Section 63-18-110.

Although the above states have chosen to require hand-on energy healing practitioners to be licensed massage therapists, other states have chosen to exempt them from needing a license to practice. Several national organizations such as the Healing Touch Professional Association and the International Society of Reiki Professionals have been able to get laws passed that exempt hands-on energy healing methods from being considered the practice of massage. As an example, below is North Dakota's law that exempts hand-on energy healing practitioners from being required to be licensed massage therapists.

North Dakota - Chapter 43-25 Massage Therapists

43-24-04 Exemptions. The following persons are exempt from this chapter...6. Any individual practicing healing by manipulating the energy field or the flow of energy of the human body by means other than the manipulation of the soft tissues of the human body, provided that the individual's services are not designated or implied to be massage or massage therapy. For purposes of this subsection, a light touch or tap is not a manipulation of the soft tissues of the human body.

Based on the foregoing, it is important to determine of you need to be a licensed massage therapist in your state in order to offer energy healing methods that include touch to the public.

A word of caution about using touch with patients for licensed mental health care professionals: There are laws and regulations governing licensed mental health care practitioners that expressly prohibit the practitioner from touching a patient. This prohibition was enacted because practitioners were inappropriately touching patients, including engaging in sexual relationships with patients. Touching a patient can result in the practitioner being subject to professional discipline and revocation of the practitioner's license. In the field of energy psychology, it's not uncommon for licensed mental health practitioners to use muscle testing. They may even tap on a patient if the patient is not able to perform the tapping. If you are in this category, make sure you have in your Informed Consent, Agreement for Psychotherapy Services 1) language explaining the theoretical basis for touching a client; 2) language granting you permission to use touch, specifically, light touch, muscle testing and tapping, and; 3) language giving the patient the right to refuse being touched.

Malpractice and negligence

MALPRACTICE IS TYPICALLY DEFINED AS unskillful practice that fails to conform to a standard of care in the profession and results in client injury (Cohen, 2003). As stated earlier, standards of care are specific to a profession (e.g. medicine, psychology, acupuncture, counseling, etc.). Therefore, licensed providers can be sued for malpractice by patients and also can be subject to professional discipline based on a malpractice claim. Most people are familiar with surgeons being sued for malpractice because they left a surgical instrument or sponge in a patient. This is a clear example of an unskillful practice that fails to conform to the surgeon's standards of care resulting in harm to the patient. Another example of malpractice would be if an acupuncturist used tainted needles and the patient developed an infection from the use of the tainted needles.

With regard to the non-conventional nature of energy healing methods, however, in the context of malpractice defense, there is a legal defense to medical malpractice known as the "respectable minority" doctrine. The rule essentially states that a physician, who undertakes a mode of treatment that a respectable minority within the profession would undertake under similar circumstances, does not incur liability for malpractice merely because the physician substituted such an approach for the more generally approved one.

Negligence encompasses failure to perform the duty of due care which results in injury to another. Non-licensed practitioners are subject to claims of negligence by their clients as well as other common civil torts. For example, a non-licensed energy healing practitioner could be subject to a negligence lawsuit if the practitioner, while working with a client to improve self-esteem for work advancement, failed to refer the client to a mental health care professional when the client demonstrated problematic behavior. This problematic behavior could be issues such as erratic emotions, hearing voices, having suicidal thoughts, excessive drinking or eating, depression, sleep disturbances, or other behavior that indicates serious problems in basic functioning. The court would need to determine whether the practitioner acted as a "reasonable energy healing practitioner." Failure to refer in this case, would most likely mean that the practitioner did not act reasonably and therefore, was negligent. For further information, please refer to the books written by Michael H. Cohen as listed in the reference sections. *A second basis for a claim of malpractice and negligence liability is failure to obtain adequate informed consent.*

Including conventional treatments to reduce malpractice & negligence claims

Energy healing practitioners recognize that they operate with a very different paradigm from that of conventional Western licensed health care professionals. The theoretical basis of energy-oriented approaches suggests the reality of the human vibrational matrix. Some approaches include working in the quantum field where there is no time or space and all possibilities exist simultaneously. This is in direct opposition to allopathic medicine, which is based on Newtonian physics, a reductionist model of perceiving reality. There is room for both perceptions to help foster a holistic and integrative approach to health care. Research being conducted on a number of energy healing methods demonstrates that they can be effective for a variety of conditions. Some have been shown to be helpful in relieving pain, releasing trauma, reducing anxiety, and accelerating wound healing. The enthusiasm that many energy healing practitioners have for energy healing methods may result in creating "blind spots" regarding traditional treatments that can benefit clients.

It's imperative for all energy healing practitioners (licensed or non-licensed) to know that failure to ensure that clients have received adequate conventional care may lead to significant legal liability, including a malpractice or negligence claim and possible criminal prosecution.

Whether you are a licensed or non-licensed health care provider, clients could make a negligence or malpractice claim against you for not receiving adequate conventional care during their work with you. Licensed health care professionals face not only the risk of a malpractice claim from a patient but also the risk of triggering a professional disciplinary action by the practitioner's licensing board. Remember, licensing boards can take the position that energy healing methods fall below the standards of care or outside the legally defined scope of practice of the licensed profession. Therefore, it is essential for energy healing practitioners to consider the benefits of conventional treatments in developing a plan of care for their clients.

Often people seek out energy healing practitioners when they have exhausted traditional medical and psychological resources. The perceptive practitioner will try to determine what brings the person to seek the practitioner's care. The practitioner also will want to have an understanding about the person's medical and psychological issues. Some energy healing methods can cause energetically blocked areas to release and resume a healthy flow of Qi. Others may put the client in a deep state of relaxation and peace, thereby reducing stress and allowing the body's natural ability to heal to take over. This can result in symptoms being diminished or actually disappearing. Clients taking prescribed medication, who experience this phenomenon, may want to stop taking medications because they don't believe they need them anymore.

Only the prescribing health care professional can advise a client to reduce a medication or to cease taking it. If there is even a hint that a non-prescribing provider either expressly or by implication advised a client to change or stop any medication, this puts the non-prescribing provider at great legal risk.

For a non-licensed energy healing practitioner, a client not receiving adequate conventional care could result in a possible negligence lawsuit by the client. It also could result in criminal prosecution by the state. For licensed energy healing practitioners, a patient not receiving adequate conventional care could result in not only a possible malpractice lawsuit by the patient. It could also result in the practitioner's board filing charges for unprofessional conduct that could result in the loss of the practitioner's license. To protect my non-licensed clients, I always include the following language in their Client Agreement & Disclosure Statement:

> "You understand the energy healing methods I offer are not intended to be a substitute for medical or psychological treatment and they do not replace the services of licensed health care providers. You agree to consult with your licensed health care provider for any specific health care problems. In addition, you understand that any information shared during our session(s) is not to be considered a recommendation that you stop seeing any of your licensed health care providers or using prescribed medication, if any, without consulting with your licensed health care provider, even if after a session it appears and indicates that such medication or treatment is unnecessary."

Pertinent ethical and related legal questions arise when a client refuses traditional medical or psychological care and wants to be treated solely by energy healing methods. Practitioner need to know what is required under the licensing laws and regulations applicable to them in their state, province, or country. Is the practitioner being exposed to lawsuits from the client and possible criminal prosecution, if the client refuses traditional medical and psychological treatment? Since documenting that an adequate evaluation has been made is a requirement for all licensed health care professionals, it's very problematic when a patient refuses evaluation. Non-licensed energy healing practitioners need to do their utmost to prevent charges of negligence or malfeasance by including documentation of conventional therapies the client is receiving from a licensed practitioner. If a client refuses conventional medical care, the energy healing practitioner needs to discuss the dilemma openly with the prospective client and, if appropriate, obtain a written "Release of Liability & Assumption of Risk" legal agreement from the client. It is always advisable to identify for the client licensed professionals who are interested in working with non-traditionally oriented clients. While energy healing practitioners generally do not want to refuse care to a client who does not comply with a request to receive medical or psychological care, it may be the only and best option. There may be occasions when this is necessary to meet the ethic of providing the best possible care as well as to avoid legal liability.

It's vital for energy healing practitioners to develop trust and rapport with their clients as part of the informed consent process. This helps to allow the practitioner to offer the highest quality of care available. This can mean that the best care available is to refer the client to an appropriate specialist or other practitioner when the needs of the client exceed the expertise of the practitioner. It can also mean that the needs of the client are not within the legally defined scope of practice of the practitioner and a referral is not only the ethical choice it is legally mandated. Energy healing practitioners need to honor the client's need for conventional care if that is indicated through any symptom.

Obtaining professional and general liability insurance

If an energy healing practitioner is seeing clients, whether as a student, clinician, instructor or volunteer, it is highly recommended that an individual professional and general liability insurance policy be obtained. Even when an energy healing practitioner is doing a good job, there's always a risk that someone with whom the practitioner interacts will be dissatisfied. Any unhappy client or the client's family could file a claim against the energy healing practitioner. This can happen even if there is the practitioner is not at fault and there is no merit to the claim. One of the most common types of lawsuits that can be brought against energy healing practitioners is a claim of failure in the performance of professional duties, which results in harm. For non-licensed energy healing practitioners, such a claim would be negligence, and for licensed practitioners, malpractice. As stated above, a negligence or malpractice lawsuit seeks damages sustained from injury when the practitioner fails to perform the duty of due care according to established standards of conduct for the field. Without professional liability insurance, the energy healing practitioner would have to pay for legal defense fees and any potential settlement costs. That can amount to thousands of dollars and it can be mentally, emotionally, and financially devastating. It's important to understand that professional liability insurance generally covers legal claims brought against the practitioner from clients. A client could file a legal claim for negligence or for an injury sustained while in the practitioner's office or attending a class or workshop conducted by the practitioner. If a client files a lawsuit, the insurance company will take over and pay for defending the practitioner. However, professional liability insurance does not cover the practitioner if a licensing board or regulatory agency files a claim against the practitioner. For example, if a licensing board issued a fine against a non-licensed practitioner for unlawful practice, the practitioner's professional liability insurance would not cover the cost of defending the practitioner against the board or the fine imposed.

If an energy healing practitioner sees clients in a physical space, whether a business office or home office, client safety is the practitioner's responsibility. So, it's important for an energy healing practitioner to be aware of any slip and fall hazards that could impact clients. In addition, an energy healing practitioner should be aware of safety concerns around the treatment area, furniture placement, waiting room, etc. This awareness of safety also applies to the classroom setting if the energy healing practitioner offers trainings or workshops to the public.

Generally, licensed health care professionals are required to have malpractice insurance in order to maintain licensure. However, these malpractice insurance policies generally do not cover energy healing modalities. Therefore, licensed practitioners who incorporate energy healing methods into their practices should acquire a separate professional and general liability policy specifically for the energy healing methods they offer to patients.

The Healing Touch Professional Association and the Association for Comprehensive Energy Psychology both offer to their respective members professional and general liability insurance that covers a number of energy healing modalities. In addition, there is the Energy Medicine Professional Association and other organizations that offer professional liability insurance to energy healing practitioners.

Informed consent

AS STATED IN SECTION II above, a core concept of ethics in the helping professions is that the relationship is always client-centered. An ongoing robust informed consent process is essential for maintaining a client-centered practice. It is also the cornerstone for building rapport and trust with your clients. Informed consent for services is also a legal procedure to ensure that a client is competent and has voluntarily agreed to engage the services of the helping professional.

> Many practitioners are unaware that a client informed consent document is a legal agreement that not only needs to comply with applicable state laws and regulations, but it also needs to be legally sound and drafted specifically for the practitioner's practice.

Some states have laws and regulations that require licensed health care practitioners to obtain a signed informed consent agreement from each patient. The specific language and requirements differ between licensed professions and also each state's laws and regulations. This is why it's imperative that licensed health care providers carefully research the laws and regulations that apply to them regarding informed consent. If a licensed health care provider fails to obtain a signed informed consent agreement and/or fails to disclose the required information to a patient as set forth by law, the practitioner can be charged with unprofessional conduct and potentially malpractice for failure to obtain informed consent. When licensed health care providers incorporate energy healing methods, they are at a much greater risk of being charged by their licensing board with unprofessional conduct and malpractice. Having a legally sound Informed consent document that includes the use of energy healing methods is one of the best risk management strategies a licensed practitioner can put into place.

Non-licensed energy healing practitioners are not required by law to obtain a signed Client Agreement & Disclosure Statement (i.e. informed consent agreement), except in some states that have a health care freedom law. As provided above, these laws require specific disclosures that must be made by the practitioner to their clients. They also require the practitioner to keep a signed Client Agreement & Disclosure Statement from each client for a minimum number of years. For example, in California non-licensed alternative healing arts practitioners must keep a copy of the signed Client Agreement & Disclosure Statement for three years. Some non-licensed energy healing practitioners assume they are safe if they practice in a state that has a health care freedom law. However, the practitioner must fully comply with all the requirements of the law, including obtaining a signed Client Agreement & Disclosure Statement from each client, in order to be protected by the law. If they do not fully comply, they can be charged with practicing medicine without a license. Even if a non-licensed energy healing practitioner is not required by law to have a signed Client Agreement & Disclosure Statement, it's key from a risk management perspective to have one. A legally sound Client Agreement & Disclosure Statement protects both the practitioner and client.

In addition, insurance companies may require a release of liability clause be included in a written Client Agreement & Disclosure

Statement in order for the practitioner to obtain professional liability insurance. If the practitioner does not include such a release of liability clause then the insurance company will deny coverage. This will result in the practitioner having to defend the claim without insurance. Failure to obtain a written Client Agreement & Disclosure Statement can lead to claims of malpractice, negligence, misrepresentation, or other legal claims.

> Parents have the right to choose treatment modalities for their children and adolescents until the age of majority is reached. Therefore, all practitioners who work with minors must obtain a written informed consent from the minor's parents or legal guardian in order to provide services to the minor.

Many ethics codes require practitioners to obtain an informed consent agreement from each client. For example, failure to document and discuss risks and benefits as part of the informed consent process can be the basis for a malpractice or negligence lawsuit. Section V contains the basic components of a client agreement for services.

Fraud and misrepresentation

BOTH LICENSED AND NON-LICENSED PRACTITIONERS are subject to legal liability for fraud and misrepresentation in their practices. Fraud involves the knowing inducement of reliance on inaccurate or false information for the benefit of the person committing the fraud and to the detriment of the victim (Cohen, 1998). The practitioner must know the information is false, or recklessly fail to discover its veracity, and the victim must reasonably rely on the representation. A fraud claim typically opens the practitioner to the possibility of punitive damages. Fraud is harder to prove than negligence or misrepresentation, since fraud requires proving intention and recklessness.

Misrepresentation claims can arise from the practitioner committing false, misleading, and/or deceptive statements or actions. Many websites for alternative healing practitioners contain content that creates a significant risk of a claim of misrepresentation. These websites are also in violation of Federal Trade Commission (FTC) regulations and state consumer protection laws regarding advertising their services to the public. This is why it is essential that energy healing practitioners have a risk management audit of their websites. An audit provides the practitioner with edits and other advice regarding the legally problematic contents of the website. Making strategic edits to website language can make a significant difference in reducing potential legal liability. Section VI will cover in more detail misrepresentation as it applies to having a website and marketing an energy healing practice.

Confidentiality and privacy

CONFIDENTIALITY IS THE ONGOING OBLIGATION of licensed and non-licensed practitioners to keep private the information shared with them by clients during sessions. It is an obligation that exists until the client grants permission for confidentiality to be breached or a situation arises that falls within one of the exceptions to confidentiality (Cohen, 2000). However, there is a fundamental difference between the kind of confidentiality a non-licensed energy healing practitioner can promise and the confidentiality physicians, psychologist, and other certain licensed professionals can provide to clients. Generally non-licensed practitioners of the healing arts cannot promise "legal privilege" which is a more powerful kind of confidentiality.

Under basic confidentiality, practitioners are ethically obligated to not disclose information shared by the client during a session. This is generally viewed as an implied civil contract between the parties. If that obligation is written into the practitioner's Client Agreement & Disclosure Statement, which it should be, then it would be considered an express civil contract between the parties. If the non-licensed practitioner breaks the client's confidentiality, the practitioner could be civilly sued for breaking an implied contract or sued for breach of contract (i.e., the Client Agreement). However, the non-licensed practitioner would not be in violation of any law. In addition, if the non-licensed practitioner is placed under oath at a legal proceeding, a judge has the right to order the non-licensed practitioner to break the promise of confidentiality. Because the legal principle of confidentiality can be confusing and complicated, if a non-licensed energy healing practitioner is in a situation where a lawyer or court is requesting information about a client, it is advisable to consult with an attorney.

"Legal privilege" apples to those that practice a profession regulated by law which explicitly provides not only that the licensed practitioner must keep patient information confidential, but also the licensed practitioner may not be required to disclose in a court proceeding information provided to the licensed practitioner from the patient. A licensed practitioner who breaks confidentiality that is considered legally privileged can be civilly sued the same as a non-licensed practitioner. The licensed practitioner can also be subject to professionally discipline by the licensing board for unprofessional conduct. In addition, the licensed practitioner can be deemed to be in violation of the law and subject to punishment by the court. As a general rule, a judge may not order a licensed practitioner to disclose confidential information that is considered legally privileged. Historically, the law has recognized "legal privilege" regarding information disclosed by a client (or patient) for physicians, lawyers, clergy, and psychologists. In some states, legal privilege also applies to social workers, licensed professional counselors, and marriage and family therapists. Therefore, licensed practitioners need to be knowledgeable about the laws in their respective states regarding confidentiality. If they are in a situation where a lawyer or court is requesting information about a patient, they should seek the advice of an attorney.

There are exceptions to the duty of confidentiality that allow information to be disclosed without a client's express permission. For example, most licensed health care professionals must report suspected cases of elder or child abuse to legal authorities. Other exceptions include client emergency, express written waiver, and the possibility of the client being in imminent danger to self or others. Even under these exceptions, however, confidentiality should be breached to the least extent necessary to accomplish the necessary goal. Practitioners may also have a duty to breach confidentiality where it is necessary to protect third parties from potential violence or other risks posed by a client, such as infection (Schouten & Cohen, 2003).

Release of confidential information

On occasion an energy healing practitioner may need to discuss a client's care with a trainer, mentor, or other professionals. Generally, you do not need to obtain a written or verbal release to discuss a case with colleagues or a mentor provided you do not share information that would allow your client to be identified. However, if the information being shared would in any way allow your client to be identified, then before disclosing confidential information, it is advisable to have the client sign a "Release of Confidential Information" document. This document provides a written record that the client has consented to the practitioner's intent to discuss the client's care with a third party. Signed release of information forms granting the practitioner permission to release information to a specific party have become routine. Although some practitioners in the past felt comfortable obtaining verbal permission and recording it in the client's record, it is better to have a signed release from the client.

Privacy and HIPAA

State and federal statutes, including the Health Insurance Portability and Accountability Act (HIPAA), have increased the requirements for signed releases. HIPAA is a federal statute that was implemented by the U.S. Congress in 1996. It formalizes many of the pre-existing protections of medical information, which it refers to as Protected Health Information (PHI) (Schouten & Cohen, 2003). This law addresses a variety of issues related to health care, specifically regarding the electronic exchange, privacy, and security of health information. The HIPAA Privacy Rule sets standards with respect to the rights of individuals to their health information, procedures for exercising those rights, and the authorized and required uses and disclosures of such information. The Privacy Rule defines what information needs to be protected, who is authorized to access the protected health information, and delineates individuals' rights to control and access their own protected information.

The security standards in HIPAA were developed for two primary purposes. First and foremost, the implementation of appropriate security safeguards to protect certain electronic health information that may be at risk. Second, protecting an individual's health information, while permitting the appropriate access and use of that information, ultimately promotes the use of electronic health information in the industry. HIPAA guarantees individuals the right to access and request amendment of their PHI and to request an accounting of disclosures of their protected PHI.

HIPAA applies to regulated health care professionals and health care corporations ("covered entities"). Under the law, covered entities are required to disclose to all patients what can and cannot be done with their PHI. We have all received "Notice of Privacy Practices" from our physicians. Covered entities are also required under HIPAA to have in place a system of business policies that meet common sense requirements about privacy protection. These include policies for paper records and for electronic records such as a policy that files are to be kept in a secure location.

It is clear that when licensed health care providers work with patients within their scope of practice, they must comply with HIPAA because they are considered covered entities. Where things get murky is when a licensed health care provider works with clients via a distance in a separate unregulated practice. Does HIPAA apply to the licensed health care provider who has a separate unregulated practice? For example, what if a chiropractor decides to offer EFT/Tapping Coaching session to clients via distance for stress management and life strategies. The chiropractor is not providing EFT/Tapping coaching sessions as part of his chiropractic practice but only as an unregulated EFT/Tapping practitioner and coach. Would the chiropractor need to use a HIPAA compliant electronic platform for EFT/Tapping coaching sessions? If you fit into this category, where the application of HIPAA is unclear, you have a couple of options. One is to choose to be HIPAA compliant in your unregulated practice. A second option is to seek professional advice from a HIPAA specialist to determine if it is recommended to be HIPAA compliant or not.

Generally, non-licensed practitioners, who are not also practicing some other regulated profession, are not obligated to comply with HIPAA. However, the wording of HIPAA contains some ambiguity, which can create a problem for non-licensed practitioners. In some states that have enacted a health care freedom law, it is unclear whether they need to comply with HIPAA. Another example is the state of Colorado where non-licensed practitioners can register with the state as an "unlicensed psychotherapist." Do they need to comply with HIPAA? There is no authoritative answer, and it's not clear what governmental body has the authority to provide an answer.

If you are a non-licensed practitioner where application of HIPAA is unclear, you must decide how you wish to proceed. If you are unclear or want to model your practice with licensed professionals, the safest counsel is to choose to comply with HIPAA on a voluntary basis. That means client remote sessions would need to be conducted on a secured HIPAA compliant electronic platform. With the uncertainty regarding this issue, it may be advisable to seek professional advice from a HIPAA compliant specialist.

In addition to HIPAA, non-licensed practitioners need to be aware that they have a legal obligation to maintain the privacy and confidentiality of the information shared by their clients in session and to exercise due care. So, while non-licensed practitioners may not be subject to HIPAA, they face a more significant legal risk if they fail to maintain the privacy and confidentiality of clients when conducting sessions via distance. A non-licensed practitioner could face a tort claim in civil cord for breach of confidentiality, breach of the fiduciary duty, invasion of privacy or negligence. Because of the legal risks, the most prudent course of action would be to only use a HIPAA compliant electronic platform for client sessions conducted remotely. If the cost of being HIPAA compliant is prohibitive, there is a risk management strategy that can be implemented. In the confidentiality section of your Client Agreement & Disclosure Statement, include that if any communication regarding the client's session is conducted over the phone or via Zoom or another electronic platform, it is not possible to guarantee the confidentiality of the information. While this disclosure may or may not protect the non-licensed practitioner, it may help discourage a claim of breach of confidentiality by the client.

Breach of fiduciary duty

A "FIDUCIARY DUTY" IS A unique legal obligation whereby one party owes a duty of care to another to act in the best interest of that party. Bankers, attorneys, real estate agents, financial advisers and other professionals have a legal obligation to uphold the fiduciary duty with clients. As mentioned in Section II above, the fiduciary duty is based on the ethical principle of trust. Both licensed and non-licensed practitioners have a legally sanctioned fiduciary relationship with their clients. Therefore, they can be subject to legal liability for the breach of the fiduciary duty if they fail to maintain the fiduciary relationship with clients. A violation of the fiduciary duty is considered a type of tort, where the breach is specifically premised on a breach of a duty of loyalty by the practitioner to the client. The fundamental difference between a negligence or malpractice claim and a fiduciary duty claim is that the former focuses on the practitioner's duty of care, while the latter targets the practitioner's duty of trustworthy conduct. For example, when a practitioner exploits the power differential and engages in a sexual relationship with client, a client can sue the practitioner for breaching the fiduciary duty. In an actual case, a psychotherapist disclosed confidential patient information to the patient's employer. The patient sued the psychotherapist not only for breach of confidentiality and of the fiduciary duty but also for invasion of privacy.

Assault and battery

THE LEGAL DEFINITION OF ASSAULT is "creating an imminent apprehension of harm." The legal definition of battery is "physical contact without consent." Both in social situations, and when we are clients ourselves, we imply consent to a certain, socially understood level of contact. For example, strangers in a crowded subway train expect to be somewhat jostled. But other contact can be considered nonconsensual. This is particularly relevant in a therapeutic practice when nonconsensual contact could be construed as inappropriate or possible sexual misconduct (Cohen, 2003). Further, the obligation of informed consent requires the practitioner to discuss and disclose procedures that include touch, as well as their risks and benefits. Touch can be a potential problem in a healing relationship, if the client has a history of any kind of trauma around touch. Therefore, the practitioner needs to determine if the client has any misgiving, doubts, or any negative reactions to any physical touch. The practitioner should receive both verbal and written consent for touch from each client. Even if the energy healing method the practitioner uses does not involve touch, the practitioner still must be mindful about any physical contact with a client if that client does not like to be touched. A hug or arm around a shoulder could trigger a complaint from a client that the practitioner acted inappropriately. In both situations, this can leave the practitioner vulnerable to a tort claim for battery, if physical contact is used without consent and/or inappropriately.

> Because some energy healing methods include touch, it is essential for those energy healing practitioners who use touch with clients to obtain verbal and written consent when using touch or other physical contact with clients. Whereas such action was deemed battery in the past, increasingly, such violations come under the legal theory of malpractice or negligence.

Options for the legal structure of your energy healing practice

ALTHOUGH HOW YOU DECIDE TO legally structure your energy healing practice from a business standpoint is not a key legal principle, I often get this question from my clients. Unless you are an employee of a hospital, clinic, wellness center, or other organization, you need to decide how to legally structure your practice. Here are some options to consider:

A sole proprietorship is the simplest business form under which one can operate a business. The sole proprietorship is not a legal entity. The owner reports business income or losses on an individual tax return. It simply refers to a person who owns the business and is personally responsible for its debts. Therefore, the owner's personal assets are not protected against business debts, liabilities, legal claims, and obligations.

A **Limited Liability Company** ("LLC") is a non-corporate business whose owners actively participate in the organization's management and are protected against personal liability for the organization's debts, liabilities, legal claims, and obligations. An LLC is a hybrid legal entity that has both the characteristics of a corporation and of a partnership. It is, however, usually treated as a non-corporate business organization for tax purposes. The exception is that it's possible for the owner(s) of an LLC to petition the IRS and request the LLC to be treated as an S-Corporation for federal tax purposes.

A **corporation** is a legal entity that is separate and distinct from its owners. Corporations enjoy most of the rights and responsibilities that an individual possesses; that is, a corporation has the right to enter into contracts, loan and borrow money, sue and be sued, hire employees, own assets and pay taxes. The most central aspect of a corporation is limited liability. That is, shareholders have the right to participate in the profits, through dividends and/or the appreciation of stock but are not held personally liable for the company's debts.

A **partnership** is a contractual relationship between two or more persons carrying on a joint business venture with a view to profit, each incurring liability for losses and the right to share in the profits.

It is advisable to consult with your business attorney and tax advisor as to what structure is best suited for your energy healing practice.

RISK MANAGEMENT STRATEGIES

- To protect your practice, know, understand and be in compliance with the laws and regulations that apply to you and your practice. Each state is different.
- Practice only within your legally defined scope of practice.
- Seek professional advice from an attorney or risk management consultant.
- Obtain a Certificate of Completion in ethics, legal principles & risk management strategies for energy healing practitioners.
- If you are a licensed health care professional make sure you can demonstrate to your licensing board that you have significant training and are competent in the energy healing methods you use. This is best demonstrated by being certified in the energy healing methods you use and by the National Certification Center of Energy Practitioners.
- If you are a non-licensed practitioner make sure you have had significant training and are competent in the energy healing methods you use. This is best demonstrated by being certified in the energy healing methods you use and by the National Certification Center of Energy Practitioners.
- Have a legally sound informed consent and client agreement by seeking professional advice from an attorney or risk management consultant. Do not attempt to draft it yourself or borrow it from another practitioner.
- Obtain professional and general liability insurance that covers the energy healing method(s) you use with clients.
- If you are a non-licensed practitioner make sure you have licensed health care professionals you can refer your clients to when appropriate.

Section IV

Practical Considerations in Working with Clients

Now that we have covered the key ethical and legal principles applicable to energy healing practitioners, this section explores a number of practical issues that need to be considered in working with clients. From an ethical and legal perspective, it's imperative for the practitioner to assess whether it's appropriate to work with a particular client. An energy healing practitioner needs to develop discernment in selecting clients to work. This includes knowing when an individual should not be accepted as a client. Many energy healing methods can result in the client experiencing nonordinary states of consciousness. Therefore, it's critical for energy healing practitioners to acquire the skill and competence to deal with unusual states of consciousness that may occur spontaneously during an energy healing session.

Assessing a client's willingness to experience energy healing methods

Many new energy healing practitioners mistakenly believe that they can help any individual that inquires about their services. This belief is considered unethical and exposes the practitioner to potential legal liability. Seasoned practitioners know and understand that not every person who comes to their office is an appropriate candidate to become a client. In this section we will consider some key issues in assessing and selecting clients for your energy healing practice.

As stated in Section II, it's imperative during the informed consent process for the practitioner to include explaining the theoretical basis of the energy healing method(s) to the prospective client. This enables the client to make an informed decision whether to engage the services of the practitioner. Some clients seek out an energy healing practitioner out of curiosity or because they heard about the practitioner from a friend. Therefore, in addition to assessing a client's willingness to receive services, it's also imperative to determine if the energy work would be appropriate to the specific needs of the client. Despite the wide applicability of energy healing methods for many physical and emotional issues, it's necessary to go beyond a "one size fits all" kind of thinking.

Some individuals may not be ready for the non-verbal, intuitive nature of energy work. Also, they may not be ready for the increased focus on self-care that many energy healing methods want to foster. The intimate nature of energetic interactions that energy work can generate may be too intense or create dependency issues in some people. For people who are used to simply discussing a problem, energy work may create heightened sensitivities that may be difficult for the client to comprehend. Furthermore, energy healing methods may be conceptually quite foreign to an individual's way of thinking. This can be so despite a stated interested in experiencing a specific energy healing method. In addition, some people may be living with families who are drastically opposed to energy healing work. Therefore, the practitioner needs to carefully evaluate each clients' ability to integrate energy healing interventions into their daily life and family structure.

The more disempowered the client, the more care should be taken in introducing energy healing methods. Please consider asking yourself the following questions when you are considering taking on a new client:

- Is the person willing to try the energy healing method and evaluate the outcome with you?
- Is the person willing to do self-exploration?
- Is the person willing to set realistic goals?
- Is the person willing to accept referrals to other specialists or other practitioners if needed?
- Is the person willing to give you feedback directly to correct any misunderstandings?

This type of questioning will help in assessing whether the person is suitable for your energy healing practice. Your careful consideration in assessing potential clients will sort out people who are just curious or seeking an adventure rather than wanting positive change in their lives.

Selecting clients appropriate for energy healing services

ONE OF THE GREATEST CRITICISMS that has been made about energy healing methods is that they do not have criteria for selecting appropriate clients. As stated in the introduction to this section, many energy healing practitioners assume anyone can benefit from the energy methods they offer. It is accurate to say there is some value in the relaxation and peace clients can experience using energy healing methods. However, truth is that the diabetic really does need blood sugar regulation, the client with a deformed hip really needs an orthopedist, an adult ADD client may benefit from medication, and pain of unknown origin needs medical evaluation. Similarly, clients with emotional issues may respond well to energetic interventions. But many times, underlying emotional trauma requires more in-depth therapy by a skilled licensed mental health care practitioner. Ideal clients for energy healing methods can be recognized as those with:

- Intact ego-structure, good self-esteem and sense of personal identity.
- Clear intention to be helped.
- Willingness to receive energy work.

- Curiosity and interest in learning.
- Ability to help set and understand boundaries.
- Recognition of the sacred contract between practitioner and client.
- Participation in mutual goal setting.
- Willingness to give feedback and evaluate personal progress.
- Ability to recognize the resources of other practitioners, including medical and psychological professionals.

Clients who have these qualities are considered good candidates for receiving the benefits of energy healing methods. With these characteristics, the client is able to recognize that the quality of the relationship the client shares with the practitioner is part of the healing process. Some energy healing methods are transformational in nature. When this occurs, the client may experience a huge shift in world views and self-understanding. This can result in every aspect of the client's life, including physical, emotional, mental, and spiritual becoming enhanced. This perspective of healing differs greatly from the current understanding of curing in which symptom relief is regarded as the best outcome, and the patient remains a passive receiver of treatments given. Energy healing in the new paradigm can be a participatory process, a partnership, in which practitioner and client collaborate to find optimal outcomes and insights.

When an individual may not be appropriate for energy healing methods

WHILE IT'S IMPORTANT TO IDENTITY the qualities that are desirable in clients for energy healing methods, it's also important to identify characteristics that would cause a practitioner to be very cautious in selecting them for energy healing methods. Some people are not appropriate for energy healing work because their needs can be better served by other practitioners. Some of the issues energy healing practitioners should pay attention to and that can be warning signals that an individual may not be appropriate for energy work are:

- Poor reality contact.
- Confusion about self-identity, low self-esteem.
- Being scattered, spacey, and ungrounded with poor memory recall.
- Presence of severe systemic interferences that impact readiness to receive energy healing work such as severe untreated pain, allergies, sensitivities, chemical imbalances, dissociation, depression, and addictions.
- Confusion about touch, a tendency to romanticize the practitioner.
- Presence of long-standing personality disorders that can distort client perceptions.
- High dependency needs.
- Unrealistic expectations.
- Excessive attachment or transference.
- Unwillingness to participate in session planning.
- Objections to following referral suggestions.
- Desire to get better but with an underlying or subconscious agenda to not get better and remain unhealthy.

While the above list is not exhaustive, it provides the energy healing practitioner with an idea about areas for concern. Remember some people seek the services of an energy healing practitioner out of curiosity, for the novelty or because they have exhausted tradition pathways. *It's the responsibility of the practitioner to discern the needs of clients and help them set realistic goals.* Although I think energy healing practitioners can help clients who have the above-mentioned issues, I advise great caution in taking on these types of people. Mentorship and consultation are essential resources for dealing with complex clients.

Dealing with clients' non-ordinary states of consciousness

ONE OF THE ISSUES THAT most requires an energy healing practitioner's skill and competence is that of dealing with unusual states of consciousness that may occur spontaneously. This can be especially important as a client develops trust in the practitioner while experiencing ongoing energetic interventions. Some energy healing methods can cause clients to experience shifts in consciousness that can be more intense and unusual. Many energy healing methods are more intimate in nature because they engage energy fields, the transpersonal, shamanic, archetypal, or angelic realms. They also work with intuition and non-verbal and somatic aspects. In addition, clients tend to relax and breathe more deeply when experiencing energy work which can be a gateway to self- awareness and a more expanded consciousness.

In the past, psychologists explored possible alternated states of awareness that occurred when mood altering drug treatments were used. However, instead of medications, therapists began exploring ways of expanding patient self-insight by employing a number of techniques These techniques include approaches such as hypnosis, deep meditation, guided imagery, breath work, inner child work, and past life regression. Obviously, each of these methods requires extensive training and practice for therapists to develop competence. The intention in implementing these therapeutic techniques is to facilitate increased self-awareness and emotional breakthroughs for patients who have not found relief from more traditional psychotherapy.

However, many energy healing methods can result in spontaneous shifts in consciousness by the client. These spontaneous events are quite different from the intentional, skilled used of techniques applied by licensed professionals mentioned above. For one, they can happen quite unexpectedly in an energy healing session without the client's or practitioner's conscious choice. In addition, the practitioner may find that handling them effectively goes far beyond her knowledge or skill level. In her book *The Ethics of Caring*, Taylor calls these events "non-ordinary states of consciousness" that range from mild to very deep shifts in perception. They can include such phenomena:

- Reverie and daydreaming.
- Deep concentration.
- Sense of peace.
- Dissociation from the here and now, time distortion.
- Re-experiencing biographical flashbacks.
- Reliving a trauma event.
- Experiencing emotionally charged imagery or emotional flooding.
- Intense energy releases.
- Out-of- body experiences.
- Spiritual visions.
- Reliving one's birth.
- Near death experiences.
- Contact with shamanic, transpersonal, angelic or archetypal realms.
- Remembering a past life.

What is the responsibility of an energy healing practitioner in handling such a situation? How does the practitioner address client fears when these events happen? How does the practitioner bring helpful empathy to the session? How does the practitioner help the client understand the phenomena emerging without adding the practitioner's judgments or limited viewpoints? What can the practitioner do to support the client's internal process? How can the practitioner maximize the value of the experience and assist the client's integration for meaning and learning?

Maintaining ethical therapeutic relationships with clients experiencing non-ordinary states of consciousness requires practitioners to be prepared and aware. Clients may think they are going crazy or "losing it" when unusual states of consciousness happen. They may feel quite embarrassed or vulnerable when something so unexpected happens. *Energy healing practitioners have the task to help define these events as positive, transformative occurrences that are part of the client's inner healing process.* In the traditional therapeutic relationship, the practitioner directs the session based on a treatment plan. However, in an energy healing session it is more likely that the practitioner becomes a facilitator or witness instead. The practitioner's focus is to make sure the safety and confidentiality of the client is protected rather than leading or directing the session. I like to hold the image of the practitioner "holding the light" for the client as the client goes into uncharted territory. This can allow the space and time for inner processing. Toward the end of the session, the practitioner may give gentle reminders to return to the present. The ethical practitioner will always make sure there is time to debrief the inner events to integrate learning. And just as important, the practitioner will be certain the client is fully alert and able to safely transport herself before leaving the protected setting of the office.

It's essential to remember that non-ordinary states are not pathological in nature. They differ markedly from defensive patterns that function psychologically to hold in or repress the client's unconscious material. However, it's possible for a client to have a negative experience when using energy healing methods. This can happen especially if the client is emotionally fragile or suffers from a serious psychological disorder. That is why it is incumbent upon the practitioner to assess a client's readiness for energy work This includes knowing when a client is not appropriate for energy work as discussed above. A client may experience an abreaction such as psychotic break during a session. If this occurs and the practitioner is not a licensed mental health care professional, then legally and ethically the practitioner must refer the client to an appropriate professional for help. Also, if the energy healing practitioner does not have training in dealing with non-ordinary dimensions, then it's crucial for the practitioner to consult with practitioners who have skills to address more specialized areas of non-ordinary states. This is not only the client-centered choice but the inexperienced practitioner can also learn from the more skilled practitioner. The bottom line is whenever an energy healing practitioner is on uncertain ground, they should seek consultation.

If the practitioner offers energy healing methods that can result in the client experiencing non-ordinary states of consciousness, then the concept of informed consent needs to be broadened. It needs to include this possibility especially as the therapeutic relationship develops. The practitioner's intention is not to create anxiety or fear but rather to demystify the reality of such phenomena. As part of the informed consent process, it's important to mention the possibility of unusual states to the client in order to help create a climate where misunderstandings can be avoided.

Traditionally, informed consent is defined as the consent a client gives before the client undergoes the therapeutic process. Informed consent means that the client knows what the practitioner will do and how the procedure is likely to affect the client during and after the session. In non-ordinary states of consciousness, informed consent is different because these states can arise unexpectedly. It can be difficult to describe to a client the experience before it has happened. Another definition of informed consent better suited for energy healing methods is, "Informed consent is an attempt to ensure that the trust required is truly justified, that the power of the therapist is not abused intentionally or inadvertently, and that the caring of the therapist is expressed in ways that the patient clearly understands and desires." (Pope and Vasquez, 1991).

There are significant ethical concerns in addressing non-ordinary states of consciousness that can be experienced by clients. The following ethical considerations can help energy healing practitioners work with unusual states being experienced by clients:

- Set the intention to be centered, neutral, and fully present.
- Offer yourself as a compassionate and nonjudgmental presence.
- Trust the client's process when the client is in a deep, trance-like state.
- In whatever way possible, accept and empower the client.
- Offer understanding and a positive attitude regarding unusual phenomena.

- Avoid re-traumatizing the client.
- Understand you may have difficulty comprehending some clients' internal experiences.
- Support the positive intention of the client's desire to move toward growth and expansion.
- Practice only in your legally defined scope of practice.
- Practice only in your area of competence.
- Refer or seek consultation for unusual incidents or when a client needs further assistance.

From an ethical perspective, it's essential to remember clients experiencing non-ordinary consciousness can be more suggestible and less vigilant. They may also be less able to speak for themselves, and their defenses may be down. Energy healing practitioners must increase their awareness and attentiveness since any comment or gesture they make might lead the client away from her own process. Without vigilance it's easy for practitioners to inadvertently or unconsciously impose their values or to influence the client's thinking. At the same time, clients may experience stronger, more complicated transference with the practitioner. They will often want the advice or direction from the practitioner. Energy healing practitioners are challenged with the fine distinction between directing a session to simply holding a safe space for clients to do their internal work. The caregiver's role when a client experiences a non-ordinary state of consciousness in sessions is to empower and follow the client's process not preempt it with the caregiver's own agenda (Taylor).

Touch is always a concern in therapeutic ethics. Although most counseling disciplines advise against touch and some mental health care practice acts prohibit it, touch is often essential when working with clients in altered states. As part of the informed consent process, it's a good idea for practitioners to discuss touch with clients. The practitioner should have an understanding of and make an agreement with the client about non-verbal signaling and touch ahead of time. That way the practitioner knows the client's wishes.

Quality of touch is also an ethical issue. It's essential for the practitioner to have unconditional positive regard for the client, which is both personal and impersonal at the same time. A client knows when the touch of a practitioner is not authentic.

Section V

Client Agreement for Services (Informed Consent)

IN THIS SECTION YOU WILL learn the basic components of a Client Agreement for Services (i.e. informed consent document). As stated above, many practitioners are unaware that an informed consent document is a legal agreement. The Client Agreement for Services not only needs to comply with applicable state laws, but it also needs to be legally sound and drafted specifically for the practitioner's practice. For licensed practitioners, I recommend calling the informed consent document Informed Consent & Agreement for Services. This is the traditional document description for licensed providers. For non-licensed practitioners, I recommend they have a Client Agreement & Disclosure Statement instead of an Informed Consent & Agreement for Services. This is because a licensing board or regulatory agency may perceive that the non-licensed practitioner is providing licensed health care services if they have an Informed Consent & Agreement for Services. So, calling their informed consent document a Client Agreement & Disclosure Statement is less risky. The following are the essential components an Informed Consent & Agreement for Services or Client Agreement & Disclosure Statement:

- Description of services provided; this is unique to each practitioner.

- Theoretical basis of the energy healing methods used in your practice.
- Disclosure that energy healing methods are considered experimental and *alternative* or *complementary* to the healing arts that are licensed in your state, province, etc.
- Risks and benefits, without this the document is legally insufficient.
- Limitations of practice, especially for non-licensed practitioners.
- Nature of relationship Psychotherapist? Coach? Intuitive healer? Spiritual Mentor?
- Client's right to terminate sessions at any time.
- Assumption of risk legal language.
- Release of liability legal language.
- Standard office policies and procedures, fees, payment, cancellation policy, etc.
- Confidentiality, when by law you may have to disclose information.
- Education and training of practitioner.
- Acknowledgement and consent to receive services legal language.

As stated in the previous section, some states have laws requiring a practitioner to obtain a signed agreement from each client which contains specific disclosures. Because California is a state that has enacted a health care freedom law, here is sample language that a non-licensed alternative healing arts practitioner must have in a Client Agreement & Disclosure Statement in order to comply with California law:

Although I am a certified Eden Energy Medicine practitioner, I'm not licensed in the State of California as a physician, psychologist, or other licensed health care provider, nor are my services licensed by the State of California. Under Sections 2053.5 and 2053.6 of California's Business and Professions Code, I can offer you my services, subject to the requirements and restrictions that are described fully therein.

Remember, failure to obtain a written Client Agreement (i.e. informed consent document) can lead to claims of malpractice, negligence, misrepresentation, or other legal claims.

RISK MANAGEMENT STRATEGIES

- To protect your practice, know, understand, and be in compliance with the laws and regulations in your state regarding informed consent and client agreements.
- Seek professional advice in creating your Informed Consent & Agreement for Services or Client Agreement & Disclosure Statement, whichever is applicable to you. It needs to be legally sound and it should be written and designed specifically for your practice. You are unique!
- Do not attempt to draft your own Informed Consent & Agreement for Services or Client Agreement & Disclosure Agreement, use a generic form, get it out of a book, or borrow an informed consent or client agreement from another practitioner. Those forms will not legally protect you!

Section VI

Marketing Your Energy Healing Practice – Websites

MOST PRACTITIONERS USING INNOVATIVE ENERGY healing methods are not aware of the various legal issues that impact and govern their ability to represent themselves to the public via their websites. There are a number of ways that both licensed and non-licensed energy healing practitioners can find themselves in costly and debilitating legal dilemmas. Practitioners can incur legal liability because of the title they use, how they describe their services and what is published on their website. In fact, more than 95 percent of the websites marketing the services of energy healing practitioners are at significant risk of having a legal claim filed against them. Many energy healing practitioners think they are safe because their websites are similar to all the others. This is unwise and contributes to the prevailing perception that the practice of energy healing methods in the United States is akin to the "wild, wild, West." Mainstream health care has this perception because the practice of energy healing methods is currently not regulated and anyone can identify and represent themselves as an energy healing practitioner. Again, this is why becoming certified by the National Certification Center of Energy Practitioners (NCCOEP) is critical for energy healing methods to gain acceptance within mainstream health care.

It's important to be aware that there are actual situations where cease and desist letters have been sent by various licensing boards against energy healing practitioners. This was not because a formal complaint was received by the board from a client but solely because of the content of their websites. The consequences of receiving a cease and desist letter from a licensing board vary depending on the nature of the complaint from the board. It could be a reprimand, a citation with a substantial fine, or it could result in an order of closure for the practice. Practitioners have the right to hire an attorney to defend themselves. However, because legal fees amount to thousands of dollars, most do not have the financial resources to hire an attorney.

Many energy healing practitioners could unknowingly be in violation of their state laws, including consumer protections laws and their medical and/or psychotherapy practice acts. Many energy healing practitioners are completely unaware that health care licensing statutes only allow licensed practitioners to use certain titles. Practitioners can get into trouble by using a protected or restricted title or describing their services in violation of the laws and regulations that apply to them. This sends up a red flag to a licensing board that can result in an investigation by the board. Please be aware that state licensing boards are routinely looking at websites and targeting those practitioners that are in violation of the law. This applies to both licensed and non-licensed practitioners and covers all professional health care practitioners.

In addition to licensing boards, energy healing practitioners also could unknowingly be in violation of Federal Trade Commission (FTC) regulations. FTC regulations are promulgated to prevent fraud, deception, and misleading and unfair business practices in the marketplace. The FTC pays closest attention to ads and websites that make claims about health and safety. It has put together a task force to review websites offering health care products or services that make questionable claims of curative ability, are exaggerated, or unproven. The FTC is specifically targeting "newly discovered" therapies that claim to help cure a wide range of ailments. Practitioners can significantly reduce their risk of having a run-in with a licensing board or receiving a complaint from the FTC by conducting a risk management audit of their website and other marketing materials. Also, besides FTC regulations, energy healing practitioners are also subject to having a claim brought against them for misleading or deceptive advertising under their state consumer protection laws.

Misleading claims that energy healing methods are evidence-based

MANY PRACTITIONERS MAKE CLAIMS ON their websites that the energy healing methods they use are evidence-based. This predominantly comes from practitioners that use methods such as Emotional Freedom Techniques (EFT) and its precursor, Thought Field Therapy (TFT). This is because there is published research on the efficacy of these methods for certain psychological disorders. However, in order for new innovative therapies such as TFT and EFT to be accepted by the government, they must be considered evidence-based practices. What does evidence-based mean? According to the Oregon Research Institute, "An evidence-based practice is a practice that has been rigorously evaluated in experimental evaluations – like randomized controlled trials – and shown to make a positive statistically significant difference in important outcomes." With respect to EFT, practitioners can say that EFT is scientifically valid and it meets the criteria to be considered evidence-based. However, until recently, to officially be called evidence-based, the treatment must be listed on the National Registry of Evidence-based Programs and Practices (NREPP), a searchable online database of mental health and substance abuse interventions.

The NREPP was part of the US government's Substance Abuse and Mental Health Services Administration (SAMHSA). In 2016, TFT had been listed by the NREPP as an evidence-based treatment for trauma and stress-related disorders and symptoms. Because EFT is based on TFT and there has been substantial research published on EFT, it was hoped that EFT would soon also be officially listed.

But in 2018 the Assistant Secretary for Mental Health and Substance Abuse and SAMSHA phased out the NREPP website, which had been used since 1997. Since EFT had not been listed in the NREPP before that program was taken down, it is not yet officially considered an evidence-based treatment. Also, when the NREPP was taken down, the path for EFT to become officially accepted as evidence-based is now blocked. Unfortunately, as of February 2020, on the new Evidence-based Practices Resource Center website neither TFT or EFT are listed as evidence-based treatments.

The bottom line is that no energy healing method has been officially accepted by the government as an evidence-based practice. Therefore, when practitioners state on their websites their methods are evidence-based, it exposes them to legal liability. For instance, the FTC would consider such a statement to be unsubstantiated, misleading, and potentially fraudulent. If a licensed practitioner were to put on her website that the energy healing method offered is evidence-based, it could subject the practitioner to professional discipline. It's important to remember that by and large, energy healing methods are considered experimental and unsubstantiated by licensing boards, regulatory agencies, and courts of law. Therefore, energy healing methods are currently not part of an established "standards of care" or "scope of practice" in any licensed health care profession. Consequently, at this time, even if you believe that energy healing methods are helpful therapeutic tools, the powers that be, by and large, do not.

> It's imperative to be aware of how energy healing methods are perceived by the authorities, because it directly impacts your ability to do your healing work in the world.

Being in violation of licensing statutes

FOR PURPOSES OF ILLUSTRATION, I'M going to focus primarily on the practice of medicine and psychotherapy, but the principles and issues discussed below generally apply to all licensed health care professionals. All fifty states license the practice of medicine and psychotherapy. One area of significant risk you face if you are a non-licensed practitioner using energy healing methods with clients is to be in violation of your state's medical or psychotherapy practice acts. This is the case unless your state provides exemptions and/or exceptions for non-licensed practitioners. Licensed health care professionals who use energy healing methods also face the risk of violating their licensure laws and regulations by using an unsubstantiated therapy with patients. So obviously, it is imperative to do some careful legal research to make sure you are not inadvertently violating your state's laws and regulations.

As a general rule there are two components to the laws that govern the practice of medicine and psychotherapy. One is the title portion of the law that prohibits the use of certain titles unless the practitioner is licensed under the law. For example, a non-licensed practitioner would be in violation of the title portion of the law of all 50 state psychology practice acts, if the practitioner used the title "Energy Psychology Practitioner". That's because only licensed psychologists can use the word "psychology" in a title. The other component is the definition of the practice of medicine and psychotherapy. For example, a non-licensed practitioner would be in violation of the definition of the practice of psychotherapy, if he advertises that he "treats clients suffering from PTSD". The licensing board would find the practitioner had violated the definition portion of the law and was practicing psychotherapy without a license.

Title – what you call yourself

Generally, state medical practice acts restrict the use of the word "physician" to only those individuals who have obtained a license to practice medicine. Energy healing practitioners aren't likely to use the title "physician" so aren't violating this part of the statute. However, words of caution for those practitioners that have PhD's and use the title of "Doctor" or any abbreviation thereof in representing themselves. They could possibly be in violation of their state medical practice act. For example, in Oregon, it's considered to be practicing medicine if a person

> "*uses the word "Doctor"...or any abbreviation or combination, thereof,...in connection with the name of the person, or any trade name in which the person is interested in the conduct of any occupation or profession pertaining to the diagnosis or treatment of human diseases or conditions mentioned in this section" (ORS 677.085).*

Therefore, it's important to be careful when listing your credentials. For example, if you are a non-licensed energy healing practitioner with a PhD, it's essential to disclose on your website and other marketing materials in what discipline you earned your PhD. It's also important to state that you are not a licensed physician, psychotherapist, or other licensed health care professional. Otherwise, it would be easy for the public and a licensing board to perceive that you are a licensed health care provider when you offer energy healing methods to the public.

Generally, state psychology practice acts restrict the use of the words "psychology," "psychologist," or "psychological" to only those individuals who have obtained a license to practice psychology. As an example, according to Oregon law, only licensed psychologists may represent themselves to be a psychologist. That seems pretty simple and straight forward. But what does that mean? In Oregon it *"means to use any title or description of services incorporating the words "psychology," "psychological," "psychotherapy" or "psychologist,"* (ORS 675.020). This is typical in many states.

The restriction in the use of certain titles also applies to other licensed mental health care practitioners such as social workers, marriage and family therapists, and professional counselors. In addition, energy healing practitioners can inadvertently violate other licensing statutes by using a legally prohibited title. For example, in some states only licensed nutritionists or registered dietitians can use the words "nutrition" or "nutritionist" in a title.

Legally problematic title examples

For purposes of illustration of how the use of certain titles can create potential legal liability, here are some examples. Please keep in mind there may be exemptions or exceptions in certain states.

"Sue Jones, Meridian Tapping Psychotherapist"
Because Sue is not a licensed psychotherapist, she is in violation of the title portion of the psychotherapy practice acts in her state for using the word "psychotherapist" in her title. This subjects her to being charged with the crime of practicing psychotherapy without a license. In addition, Sue's clients could be misled and think that she is a licensed mental health care practitioner because she uses the word "psychotherapist" in her title. This could result in a civil lawsuit from a client for misrepresentation or potentially fraud.

"Jane Doe, Master Energy Therapist"
Most psychotherapy practice acts do not specifically restrict use of the word "therapist," in a title. However, it is highly recommended that Jane, as a non-licensed practitioner, not use the word "therapist" in her title. This is because the mental health care licensing boards in her state could determine that by using the title of "therapist", Jane is engaging in the unlawful practice of psychotherapy. In addition, Jane's clients could be misled and think that Jane is a licensed mental health care practitioner because she uses the word "therapist" in her title. This could result in a civil lawsuit from a client for misrepresentation or potentially fraud.

"John Smith, Medical Intuitive"
Generally, the title portion of most medical practice acts do not specifically restrict use of the word "medical" in a title. However, when John uses the word "medical" in his title,

it could be perceived by a medical licensing board that he is offering licensed medical services. Therefore, to reduce John's potential for being charged with the crime of practicing medicine without a license, he would need to make specific disclosures. These disclosures should include statements such as that John is not a licensed physician, does not provide medical diagnosis or treatment, and his services are not licensed by the state. Further, these disclosures should be included on his website and in his Client Agreement & Disclosure Statement.

"Robert Adams, PhD, Comprehensive Energy Psychologist"
Although Dr. Adams has an academic PhD in psychology, he is not a licensed psychologist. Therefore, he would be in violation of his state's psychology practice act for using the word "psychologist" in his title. This subjects him to being charged with the crime of practicing psychology without a license. As with the examples of Jane Doe and Sue Jones, clients could be misled and think that Robert is a licensed psychologist because he uses the word "psychologist" in his title and has a PhD in psychology. This could result in a civil lawsuit from a client for misrepresentation or potentially fraud.

"Cindy Parsons, Spiritual Counselor"
In some states, such as New Jersey, Cindy would be prohibited from using the title of "counselor" unless she was a licensed mental health care professional. In other states such as Oregon, Cindy can legally use the title of "counselor". Obviously if Cindy is located in New Jersey, she would be in violation of the title portion of the law. But if Cindy is only practicing in Oregon, she would not be in violation of the title portion of the law. However, as with many non-licensed practitioners, what if Cindy offers her services across state lines. Then it would be advisable for her to not use the word "counselor" in her title. First, she would definitely be in viola-

tion of New Jersey law. Second, other states' mental health care licensing boards could determine that by using the title of "counselor", Cindy is practicing psychotherapy without a license. In addition, clients could be misled and think Cindy is a licensed mental care practitioner because she uses the word "counselor" in her title. This could result in civil lawsuit from the client for misrepresentation and potentially fraud.

"Mary Thompson, Licensed Energy Psychologist"
Although Mary is a licensed psychologist, her state does not recognize "energy psychology" as a branch of psychology. Therefore, under Mary's licensing rules and regulations, she would be prohibited from identifying herself as an "energy psychologist". By using this title, Mary could possibly be subject to professional discipline for violating her licensure rules and regulations. However, Mary may be able to disclose that she has been trained in energy psychology therapies and incorporates them in her practice.

"Don Edwards, EFT Nutrition Coach"
In some states, such as Iowa, Don would be legally prohibited from using the word "nutrition" in his title unless he was a registered dietitian. In other states such as California, Don does not need to be licensed to use the word "nutrition" in his title. Obviously if Don is located in Iowa, he would be in violation of the title portion of the law. But if Don is only practicing in California, he would not be in violation of the law because California does not regulate the practice of nutrition. However, what if Don offers his services across state lines, then it would be advisable for him to not use the word "nutrition" in his title. Because in those states that require licensure to provide nutritional services, Don could be charged with the crime of practicing nutrition without a license.

As from the above discussion, it's clear that it's imperative to do some careful legal research regarding what title you want to use for your practice. Remember, if you work with clients across state lines, you are not only subject to the laws and regulation in your state but also the laws and regulations in the state in which your client resides. State licensing boards routinely investigate websites to ensure practitioners are not violating the law. This includes checking to see if the practitioner is using a legally protected title. Licensing boards do not hesitate to go after practitioners who live in other states but offer their services across state lines.

What about using the word "healer" in a title?

I would advise you not to use the word "healer" as a title because it can be perceived that you are practicing medicine without a license. There is legal precedent for being convicted of the crime of practicing medicine without a licensed for using the title of "healer". A less risky option would be to use the word "healing" in a title, such as "Energy Healing Practitioner". To reduce the risk, it's essential on your website and in your Client Agreement & Disclosure Statement that you state that using energy healing methods is not to be construed as the practice of medicine. I'm comfortable with the risk and have chosen to use the title "Energy Healing Practitioner". Here is a sample of the language that can be incorporated into your Client Agreement & Disclosure Statement to protect yourself from the perception that you are practicing medicine when using energy healing methods with clients.

While I have extensive experience as an energy healing practitioner, I'm not a physician, psychologist, psychotherapist, or other licensed health care provider nor are my services licensed by the State of Oregon. Although energy healing methods are intended for "healing", it is not to be construed that the use of energy healing methods is the practice of medicine, psychology, psychotherapy, or other licensed health care practice. Instead I offer my services to clients with the intention to assist them in restoring balance and energetic flow in the body; thereby, creating the opportunity for the mind/body to heal naturally. You understand there is a distinction between "healing" use energy healing methods and the practice of any licensed health care practice.

What titles are less risky to use?

When I consult with a new client regarding risk management for an energy healing practice, one of the first things we discuss is what title the practitioner uses or would like to use. As a general rule, using the word "practitioner" as part of a title is safe. As stated above, I would advise not using the words "psychotherapist", "therapist", or "healer". Depending on the state in which the practitioner practices, using the word "counselor" as part of a title may or may not be legal. If my client works with individuals across state lines, as many energy healing practitioners do, then I advise my clients not to use the word counselor as part of a title. There are a number of unprotected titles that are not subject to regulation such as "coach," "mentor," "facilitator," or "educator". Some sample titles, depending on the nature of the services provided by the energy healing practitioner, that would be considered less risky are:

- Energy Balancing Coach.
- Intuitive Fertility Educator.
- Shamanic Practitioner.
- Spiritual Healing Mentor.

One of the best approaches to choosing a title is to use the credentials you have earned as an energy healing practitioner. However, please remember that having a credential or being a certified practitioner of a particular modality is not a license to practice. Here are some sample titles:

- Certified EFT Practitioner
- Certified Emotion Code Practitioner
- Certified Healing Touch Practitioner
- Certified Eden Energy Medicine Practitioner
- Reiki Master

Definition of the practice of medicine – how you describe your services

In addition to title issues, all practitioners using energy healing methods are subject to legal problems if the description of their services on their websites violates the "practice definition" of any laws that apply to licensed health care professionals. One of the most obvious health care professionals would be a "physician", but it also includes laws governing psychologists, social workers, professional counselors, marriage and family therapists, body workers, nurses, and dietitians/nutritionists. This section specifically discusses the practice of medicine. In the next section I will address the practice of psychotherapy.

Over the last one hundred years there have been numerous cases adjudicated about what constitutes the practice of medicine. These cases are helpful in our inquiry as to whether or not practicing energy healing methods could be considered the practice of medicine. There have been a few cases dealing with alternative practitioners where their criminal convictions for the unlawful practice of medicine were upheld. For example, in a 1912 case (People v. Smith), a defendant who purported to cure diseases by "laying on hands" was convicted for practicing medicine without a license. He was convicted even though he did not share with clients what was the matter with them, did not have an official office but practiced out of a home, and used only his hands. The court emphasized that a public health statute must be construed liberally. The Smith court decided the "practice of medicine" to mean "the practice of the healing art commercially, regardless of the curative agency employed." While this is an old case, it is typical of decisions made by courts in other jurisdictions. Because state medical practice acts have been so broadly construed by the courts, they have basically created for MD's a monopoly over the practice of medicine in the United States. With substantial legal precedence behind them, they assert that any healing modality, present or future, must come within the sphere of "medicine." Consequently, judicial opinions regarding alternative healing arts practitioners reflect the dominance of the medical profession over the delivery of health care in the United States. It also significantly substantiates the risk of alternative healing arts practitioners being charged with practicing medicine without a license. Because of this significant risk, a few states have enacted health care freedom laws. As provided in Section III, these laws protect alternative healing arts practitioners from being charged with practicing medicine without a license. However, as previously stated, the vast majority of states have not enacted a health care freedom law. Therefore, the risk is significant.

As an example, in Oregon the "practice of medicine" is defined as to *"offer or undertake to diagnose, cure or treat in any manner, or by any means, methods, devices or instrumentalities, any disease, illness, pain, wound, fracture, infirmity, deformity, defect or abnormal physical or mental condition of any person."* (ORS 677.085(4). Unfortunately, the laws that govern the practice of medicine and how those laws have been interpreted by the courts are antiquated. They are based on a 19th century regulatory paradigm that doesn't fit into the expanded use of energy healing methods as part of the health care industry in this country. Nevertheless, even though the mainstream health care field does not does not embrace energy healing methods, all energy healing practitioners must still operate within the current legal and regulatory system.

Historically, physicians have customarily used certain terminology to describe their profession and its purposes. Some of these are "consult with patients," "treatment of disease or illness," "prescribe remedies," "diagnose illness," "cure illness," "provide therapy," "administer medicine," and "relieve symptoms of illness." These are terms and terminology that non-licensed practitioners must avoid using when describing their services on their websites or other marketing materials. The mere fact that a non-licensed practitioner has published any of these terms on a website can be prima face evidence that the practitioner is practicing medicine without a license.

Many non-licensed practitioners state in their marketing materials that their energy healing services can help client dealing with physical pain. While the word "pain" seems to be generic, it is not. The Federal Trade Commission (FTC), medical licensing boards, and courts have determined that "pain" is a medical condition. Consequently, it raises a red flag by using the word "pain" on a website. A non-licensed practitioner can be in jeopardy of being charged with the unlawful practice of medicine. Instead of using the word "pain", it's recommended that non-licensed practitioners use the words "physical discomfort" instead of "pain" There are other words and phrases such as "allergies" and "weight loss" that can raise a red flag. So again a risk management audit of your marketing materials is highly advisable.

It's not only non-licensed practitioners that face legal risks regarding the practice of medicine but physicians as well. All physicians must comply with the "standards of care" and "scope of practice" as defined by their respective licensing laws, regulations, and administrative rules. As I mentioned in Section III, energy healing methods are considered experimental, and they have not been substantiated by mainstream medicine. Consequently, they are deemed to be outside the traditional standards of care and scope of practice definitions that all physicians must follow in treating patients. Physicians could be subject to professional discipline for advertising they use for energy healing methods with patients. This is because it could be determined that these methods are per se outside the scope of practice or fall below the standards of care. Physicians face the risk of being subject to professional discipline by their respective medical board for advertising they offer energy healing methods to patient. This risk can be managed by having a legally sound website disclaimer and website audit provided by a risk management consultant or attorney knowledgeable about energy healing methods.

For example, a physician who is certified in the method called Matrix Energetics, received a demand letter from her medical board. The board was concerned about her use of Matrix Energetics in her practice. The medical board had received a complaint from a visitor to her website about offering Matrix Energetics as part of her medical practice. The physician had to hire a local attorney to handle her defense with the medical board. I conducted a website audit and revised her Patient Informed Consent Agreement to reduce future potential legal problems. Fortunately, our combined efforts to help her resulted in the medical board not taking any further action. If we had not been successful, the physician faced the risk of having her license suspended or of having to eliminate Matrix Energetics from her practice. In the worst-case scenario, she could have lost her license to practice medicine. As mentioned in Section III some states have passed legislation that protects physicians from facing professional discipline for practicing complementary or alternative medicine.

Definition of the practice of psychology – how you describe your services

As with the practice of medicine, many practitioners using energy healing methods are subject to legal problems if on their websites the description of their services violates the definition of the "practice of psychology" or other mental health care practice acts.

In one case a non-licensed practitioner was deemed to be representing herself as a psychologist in violation of the law. This was because she posted on her website that she used energy psychology methods as part of the services she provided to her clients as a spiritual counselor. She found herself in legal trouble because she used the word "psychology" in the description of her services. Another non-licensed practitioner advertised on his website that he "treats emotional issues". He received a citation and a several thousand dollar fine from the Psychology Board in his state. This is because using the word "treats" to describe his services was perceived to be the practice of psychotherapy. The end result is that he had to close his energy healing practice.

To further explore the definition of the practice of psychology, again as an example, in Oregon the law states that the *"Practice of psychology means rendering or offering to render supervision, consultation, evaluation or therapy services to individuals, groups or organizations for the purpose of diagnosing or treating behavioral, emotional or mental disorders." (ORS 674.010)* This is a very broad definition. Historically the courts have ruled that psychology boards have broad discretionary powers in determining the meaning of the practice of psychology. Consequently, like with the practice of medicine, judicial opinions regarding the practice of psychology and psychotherapy have not been favorable to energy healing practitioners.

Because of the laws governing the practice of psychology and psychotherapy, non-licensed practitioners need to be aware of the *Diagnostic and Statistical Manual for Mental Disorders, Edition 5* (DSM-5). As stated in Section III, the DSM-5 defines all the major categories of mental illness. As a general rule only licensed mental health care professionals can consult, evaluate, treat, and/or diagnose psychological disorders listed in the DSM-5. There are a few exceptions like the State of Colorado. Colorado allows non-licensed practitioners to practice psychotherapy provided they register and comply with the regulations promulgated by the Colorado Department of Regulatory Agencies. Therefore, it's imperative to know the laws in your state.

Based on the foregoing, it's advisable for non-licensed practitioners to not represent on their websites or in other marketing materials that they help clients with anxiety, PTSD, phobias, trauma, anxiety or depression. This is because these are all considered psychological disorders as listed in the DSM-5. Unless there are exemptions in the non-licensed practitioner's state, the practitioner faces the risk of being charged with practicing psychology or psychotherapy without a license. So, it's essential for non-licensed practitioners to not use words in marketing materials that are considered psychological disorders. Also, it's important to disclose that the non-licensed practitioner is not a licensed mental health care provider. Furthermore, the non-licensed practitioner should disclose that the use of energy healing methods with clients is not to be construed as the practice of psychotherapy and they are not a substitute for psychotherapy services. In addition, it's advisable for the non-licensed practitioners to disclose the purpose of the services they offer using energy healing methods. For example, for personal development, spiritual transformation, stress management, life coaching, or for balance and relaxation. These disclosures should be part of the non-licensed practitioner's website disclaimer and also included in the Client Agreement & Disclosure Statement.

As stated before, it's also advisable for non-licensed practitioners to not use the words "therapy" or "therapies" in describing their services on websites and other marketing materials. The reason is a licensing board would have the perception, and also the public, that by using the words "therapy" or "therapies", the non-licensed practitioner is providing licensed health care services. So, these words are misleading if used by a non-licensed practitioner. This creates the risk of a being charged with practicing a licensed profession without a license. In addition, it creates the risk of a civil lawsuit for misrepresentation by clients and also visitors to the non-licensed practitioner's website.

It's not only non-licensed practitioners that face legal risks but also licensed mental health care professionals. Like physicians, all licensed mental health care professionals must comply with the standards of care and scope of practice as defined by their respective licensing laws, regulations, and administrative rules. As I previously mentioned, energy healing methods are considered experimental and unsubstantiated by the mainstream mental health care field. Consequently, they are deemed to be outside the traditional standards of care and scope of practice definitions that all licensed mental health care professionals must follow in treating patients. Licensed mental health care professionals could be subject to professional discipline by their respective licensing board for advertising they use energy healing methods with patients. This is because their licensing board could determine that using energy healing methods is per se malpractice and outside the scope of practice or falls below the standards of care. Licensed mental health care professionals face the risk of suspension, having to eliminate energy healing methods from their practices and/or losing their licenses when they advertise energy healing methods on a website or in other marketing materials. This risk can be managed by having a legally sound website disclaimer and website audit provided by a risk management consultant or attorney knowledgeable about energy healing methods.

In one case, a licensed clinical social worker posted on her website that she used energy psychology methods in her practice. She received a complaint from her licensing board stating she was not licensed or authorized to practice psychology. Therefore, she could not offer psychology services to the public. The board had objected to her advertising that she offered energy psychology methods. The board went on to say the use of "psychology" or any other term to suggest she was authorized to practice such profession could result in charges of unprofessional conduct. She was told by the board that she could only practice licensed clinical social work as defined by the laws and regulations governing her licensure. In another case, a licensed professional counselor was using an energy healing method in her practice. She received a cease and desist letter from her board asserting she was using an unsubstantiated treatment method in violation of the regulations. The board claimed that this unsubstantiated treatment method was outside her scope of practice. After a costly legal battle, she had to cease and desist from using the energy healing method in practice. If she wanted to continue using the energy healing method, she could only use it for coaching work with clients not therapy. As I mentioned in Section III, a licensed marriage and family therapist lost her license to practice. This was because as part of her psychotherapy practice she also removed "entities" she perceived were attached to her patients.

Therefore, mental health care professionals who incorporate energy healing methods in their practices face the risk of having to defend themselves if questioned by their respective licensing board.

As mentioned above, one of best risk management strategies, among others, is for the licensed professional to have a risk management audit conducted on all marketing materials, including websites.

Description of services examples

To give you a practical idea of possible website issues, here are several examples of legally problematic description of services:

Below is language I found on an actual website of a non-licensed meridian tapping practitioner that is legally problematic:

"I specialize in helping clients recover from emotional trauma, including PTSD. I am trained in the latest cutting-edge energy psychology methods...."

The above description of services contains DSM-5 disorders (trauma, PTSD) and the word "psychology." Therefore, it's highly probable that a psychology licensing board would take the position the non-licensed meridian tapping practitioner is practicing psychology without a license. Here is a better description to reduce potential legal risks:

"I specialize in helping my clients find balance with innovative energy techniques that have been shown to help release the energetic impact of stressful life events."

Here is another example of language describing the services of a non-licensed energy healing practitioner that is legally problematic:

"As an energy healing practitioner, I treat clients that suffer from anxiety and help clients recover from long-standing panic attacks and depression with innovative energy therapies."

The above description contains DSM-5 disorders (anxiety, panic attacks, and depression) and the words "treat" and "therapies". Therefore, it's highly probable that a psychotherapy licensing board would take the position the non-licensed energy healing practitioner is practicing psychotherapy without a license. Here is a better description to reduce potential legal risks:

"As an energy healing practitioner, I specialize in using innovative energy-based techniques to help my clients experience a sense of well-being, and feel more positive, balanced, and peaceful."

Here is another example of language that would be legally problematic for a non-licensed energy healing practitioner:

"I offer a revolutionary new energy healing method that can provide relief from the symptoms of conditions such as allergies, insomnia, and back pain."

The above description contains medical conditions (allergies, insomnia, and back pain) and uses the word "symptoms.". Therefore, it's highly probable that a medical licensing board would take the position that the non-licensed energy healing practitioner is practicing medicine without a license.

> Remember licensing boards have filed complaints
> against alternative practitioners solely from
> what is published on their websites.

Risk of receiving a complaint from the Federal Trade Commission (FTC)

As MENTIONED ABOVE, THE FTC is the nation's consumer protection agency. The FTC's Bureau of Consumer Protection works for the consumer to prevent fraud, deception, and unfair business practices in the marketplace. In addition, many states have consumer protection laws which energy healing practitioners must also comply with when marketing their services on their website This is especially the case when they make claims and use client testimonials. A few years ago, the FTC put together a task force to review websites offering health care products or services that make questionable claims of curative ability, that are exaggerated, or that are unproven. The FTC is specifically targeting "newly discovered" therapies that claim to help cure a wide range of ailments. This would include all of the energy healing methods within the field of Complementary and Alternative Medicine. The FTC is checking websites looking at several items:

- The type of modality, technique, or therapy offered by the practitioner.
- The qualifications of the practitioner.
- The claims of effectiveness.
- Violations in the use of restricted language such as non-licensed practitioners using the word "treatment" or "pain" on their websites.
- Lack of scientific proof for the modality, technique, or therapy.

What are the consequences of having a complaint filed against you by the FTC based on the contents of your website? At the very least you will incur significant legal fees in answering a complaint filed against you by the FTC. Also, you could be subject to a substantial fine. As an example, in an actual case, in 1998 the FTC brought a complaint against Dr. Roger Callahan. Dr Callahan is considered a pioneer in the field of energy psychology who developed Thought Field Therapy (TFT). A Decision and Order was published by the FTC (Docket No. C-3797). The FTC determined that Dr. Callahan's Addiction Breaking System using TFT lacked competent and reliable scientific evidence among other things. Dr. Callahan and his attorneys entered into a consent order. He was fined $50,000 and was subject to a number of restrictions. Obviously, all practitioners want to avoid running afoul of the FTC.

Use of claims and testimonials – BEWARE

Most energy healing practitioners make claims about their services and publish client testimonials on their websites. They do this for the purpose of advertising and promoting their practices. However, most of these practitioners are not aware that the use of claims and testimonials in advertising must comply with FTC laws and regulations, specifically Section 5 of the FTC Act (15 U.S.C. 45). These energy healing practitioners unknowingly are violating FTC regulations and subjecting themselves to a potential complaint from the FTC because of claims and testimonials on their websites. In addition, they could be in violation of their state's consumer protection laws. Also, in the case of non-licensed energy healing practitioners, because claims and testimonials can also be descriptive of their services, they can be at risk for being charged with practicing a licensed profession without a license.

As stated at the beginning of this section, many energy healing practitioners think they are safe because their websites are similar to all the others. This is unwise. Remember licensing boards, regulatory agencies, and the courts have a negative perception of energy healing methods They consider them to be unsubstantiated, suspect, and on-the-fringe. In addition, practitioners mistakenly believe client testimonials published on their websites are protected by the First Amendment. This is not the case. If a client claims in a testimonial that an energy healing method cured a medical or psychological condition, FTC laws and regulation governing advertising would supersede the client's First Amendment free speech rights. That means that the testimonial is not protected by the First Amendment but instead is considered a form of advertising.

First, let's state the obvious. From an ethical perspective, client testimonials should be true. From a legal perspective and under FTC regulations, client testimonials must be true. Additionally, under FTC regulations, the FTC views client testimonials as claims and satisfied customers are not sufficient to support a health claim. Under the law you must have proof to back up express and implied claims on your website. In addition, health claims must be supported by *"competent and reliable scientific evidence."* Scientific evidence must be evaluated by qualified people. Research and studies must be published in peer reviewed journals and conducted using methods that experts in the field consider acceptable and accurate. What that generally means is double blind, placebo controlled, human clinical trials. Needless to say, the websites of energy healing practitioners containing health claims, by and large, do not meet the FTC's standard of being supported by competent and reliable scientific evidence.

Over 95 percent of websites featuring the services of energy healing practitioners carry significant legal risks. This risk can be managed by having a legally sound website disclaimer and a website audit provided by a risk management consultant or attorney knowledgeable about FTC regulations and energy healing.

Testimonial and claims examples

To give you a practical idea, here are several examples of legally problematic client testimonials and claims if they were published on a non-licensed energy healing practitioner's website:

"I've have been obese for many years but after getting energy healing treatments from Suzie I'm no longer obese".

This testimonial has two major problems. First, because obesity is considered a medical condition, the testimonial would be viewed as a claim that the practitioner has cured a medical condition. The FTC would require scientific evidence that Suzie's energy healing method successfully treats obesity. Second, because obesity is considered a medical condition and the testimonial uses the word "treatment," the practitioner faces of the risk of being charged with practicing medicine without a license. Here is a better way to phrase the above testimonial in order to reduce the potential legal risks:

"I've dealt with weight issues for many years, but after working with Suzie, my eating habits have improved, and I'm better able to choose foods that support my goals. I feel great and people compliment me on my appearance."

Here is another example of a legally problematic testimonial if it were to be published on the website of a Complementary and Alternative Medicine clinic that is under the direction of a licensed physician:

"I was really sick when my friend told me about the Complete Health Restoration Program. I had been dealing with the daily struggle of a progressive disease called Ankylosing Spondylitis.

The inflammation, pain and hardening of my connective tissues progressed every night as I slept. After the first round of treatments, I started to thrive. I could feel the reversal of the disease process."

Since the program is being offered under the direction of a licensed physician, the clinic is not subject to being charged with practicing medicine without a license. However, these statements could be construed by the FTC as a claim that The Completion Health Restoration Program cured a disease. In order to make such a claim, the FTC would require competent and reliable scientific evidence. Here is a better way to phrase the above testimonial in order to reduce the potential legal risks, including adding a testimonial disclaimer:

We recognize that testimonials are selective and are not fully representative of everyone's experience. We can't guarantee any specific results, and the following testimonial does not constitute a warranty or prediction regarding the outcome of an individual using our services for any particular issue. Still, we share this to give a sense of what this client has experienced.

"I began using the Complete Health Restoration Program, a complementary and alternative medicine approach to wellness, to help me to deal with inflammation and chronic and debilitating pain. After several treatments, I started to feel better and am now able to move more freely."

Here is an example of a legally problematic testimonial if it were to be published on a non-licensed energy healing practitioner's website:

"I suffered from depression and PTSD after being discharged from the military but after getting energy healing treatments from Derek, I'm no longer suffering from depression or PTSD".

This testimonial has two major problems. First, depression and PTSD are considered DSM-5 psychological disorders. These disorders, as a general rule can only be treated by licensed mental health care professionals. Therefore, the non-licensed practitioner faces of the risk of being charged with practicing psychotherapy without a license. Second, the testimonial is also considered to be a claim that the non-licensed practitioner has cured DSM-5 psychological disorders. The FTC would require scientific evidence that Derek's energy healing method successfully treats depression and PTSD. Here is a better way to phrase the above testimonial in order to reduce the potential legal risks:

> *"I have dealt with a lack a purpose and a tremendous amount of stress after being discharged from the military. After working with Derek using an innovative energy-based technique, I have experienced a greater sense of peace and well-being and feel more positive."*

Here is an example of a legally problematic claim if it were to be published on the website of a licensed psychologist:

> *"Today, a revolutionary new method called XYZ can provide relief for depression, PTSD, and any other psychological or physical problem. You can truly resolve these issues quickly and forever."*

A licensed psychologist can legally treat depression and PTSD, and use the word "psychological" on a website. However, these statements could be construed by the FTC as claims of XYZ's curative ability that requires reliable scientific evidence. Here is a better way to phrase the above claim in order to reduce the potential legal risks:

> *"XYZ is an innovative energy-based technique, and although it is still experimental, in my psychology practice clients have reported experiencing relief from negative emotions resulting in feeling more optimistic and vital."*

As you can see, there is much to consider before publishing any kind of claim or client testimonial on your website. Due to the complexity of the legal and regulatory requirements regarding claims and client testimonials, it is a good idea to seek professional help. The nuance of the words chosen can make a significant difference as to whether or not you are subjecting yourself to potential legal liability. This is why it is advisable to conduct a risk management audit of your website, especially if you make any claims or use testimonials.

Risk of a legal complaint by a visitor to your website

From a legal standpoint, what you say about yourself and your services on your website is like a binding contract with each visitor to your website. Many practitioners do not understand the legal vulnerabilities they face because of the language they use on their websites. This includes how they describe their credentials, their services, and the claims of effectiveness of the energy healing methods they offer to the public.

Many energy healing practitioners inadvertently provide legal guarantees to visitors by the language they publish on their websites. Here is an example of what I mean by "legal guarantee."

"Using XYZ in my own life helped me overcome insomnia. You will sleep better too after using XYZ."

When the practitioner used the word "will" it created a legal guarantee. This statement is also considered misleading and deceptive advertising under FTC regulations. If a visitor engaged the practitioner after reading this statement, and then did not get relief from insomnia, as promised on the website, the visitor (now client) could file a civil lawsuit. One of the legal claims the client could assert against the practitioner is misrepresentation and potentially fraud.

What legal risks you face depends on the content of your website. Many energy healing practitioners provide information, advice, and/or instructional information on their websites. This exposes them to a number of potential legal claims. For example, you could be sued for negligence if someone claimed to suffer any injury (physical, emotional, financial, etc.) because the person followed advice you provided on your website.

The risk of facing a lawsuit is greatly enhanced if you provide any instructional information about an energy healing method on your website. There are numerous energy healing methods that can be taught as self-help tools such as EFT/Tapping. What if you publish on your website how to self-administer the basic steps of EFT/Tapping? You also include the statement on your website that EFT/Tapping is a great self-help technique for relieving depression. What if your visitor suffers from severe depression and in using EFT/Tapping, as published on your website, claims that his depression got worse instead of better? What if he claims he suffered an abreaction self-administering EFT/Tapping, as taught on your website? The visitor could file a civil lawsuit against you for negligence. In addition, the visitor could claim you provided misleading information and sue you for misrepresentation and potentially fraud. Remember a claim can be made by a disgruntled visitor even if there is no merit to the claim. Nevertheless, you still have to hire a lawyer and defend the claim which can cost thousands of dollars. Also, if you are not a licensed mental health care professional, you are at risk for being charged with practicing psychotherapy without a license. This is because it could be perceived that you treat depression, a DSM-5 disorder, when you publish on your website that EFT/Tapping can relieve depression.

Given our ever-growing litigious society and the fact that energy healing methods are considered experimental by the authorities and most of the public, this only heightens your legal risks associated with having a website. Many of the potential legal issues that can arise from the misuse of language on a practitioner's website can be ameliorated by conducting an audit of your websites content and by having a legally sound disclaimer. The next section will focus on disclaimers and why a website disclaimer is an essential risk management strategy for all energy healing practitioners.

Why you need a website disclaimer

IN THIS SECTION I WILL discuss the importance of having a disclaimer on your website as an essential risk management strategy for protecting your practice. It's important to know that a website disclaimer is the legal agreement that governs the relationship between you and visitors to your website. This section will also provide some of the basic information that should be included in your website disclaimer. In addition, it explains why in order to be effective, the placement of your disclaimer on your website is critical.

First, it does not matter if you are an individual practitioner (licensed or non-licensed), part of a group practice such as a wellness or integrative care clinic, or an organization, you need a website disclaimer. A disclaimer is generally any statement intended to specify or delimit the scope of rights and obligations that may be exercised and enforced by parties in a legally-recognized relationship. Your website is like a "contract" between you and each visitor to your website, thus you become legally obligated and "contractually" bound by what you publish on your website. Another way to look at your disclaimer is that it's a type of "informed consent" for each visitor. By posting your disclaimer prominently and by having the specific legal language you need for your website, the viewer agrees to the terms of the disclaimer.

Even though a disclaimer provides no guarantee of any shield from liability, you still need a disclaimer so as to be able to at least have some claim to a defense. There is a recently published case in New Zealand (Patchett v SPATA) where a visitor to the SPATA website filed a claim of negligence; the court found SPATA's disclaimer was effective in protecting SPATA from liability.

There is no "standard" language that applies to disclaimers. Each disclaimer must be tailored to include precise language to fit the specifics of the website both in terms of the substance of the material and how it is intended to be used. General language will not suffice. An appropriate disclaimer has many elements depending on the nature of the website and the contents thereof. Some of the key components that should be included in a website disclaimer are:

- State that all information is educational in nature and is provided only as general information and is not medical or psychological advice; and

- State there is no existence of a professional relationship between the practitioner and visitor; and
- Provide that testimonials do not constitute a guarantee, warranty, or prediction regarding the outcome of an individual using any material contained herein for any particular purpose or issue; and
- Provide release of liability language stating the practitioner accepts no responsibility or liability whatsoever for the use or misuse of the information contained on the website, including links to other resources; and
- Provide an assumption of risk legal language clause; and
- Provide release of liability, indemnification, and hold harmless legal language clause; and
- State if any court of law rules that any part of the disclaimer is invalid, the disclaimer stands as if those parts were struck out.
- State by continuing to explore this website, you represent you have read, understand and agree to the terms of the disclaimer.

Not only is the content of your disclaimer important but also the placement of it on your website is crucial. You could have a legally sound disclaimer, but if it isn't positioned correctly on your website, it can be rendered meaningless. Ideally, the disclaimer should be a portal through which the visitor must pass to access the contents of your website. This means that visitors must be instructed to read and agree to the disclaimer before exploring your website. This act forms the basis to argue that the visitor entered into a "contract" with the publisher of the website. This act of entering into a contract includes that the visitor used the information on the website with full knowledge of (informed consent) and agreement with (contract) the disclaimer. If it is merely tucked off into some inconspicuous link that can be easily bypassed by the visitor, it will not protect you! The website disclaimer needs its own page and navigation tab on the website. Generally, most websites for energy healing practitioners have navigation tabs for various pages such as "home", "about", "services offered", and "contact". It also needs a navigation tab for the disclaimer page. Also, on the top of the home page of a website, the following language should be included, "Welcome…please read my disclaimer". It is advisable to place a link to the disclaimer page under the word "disclaimer". The reason for the foregoing is because FTC regulations require that disclaimers must be clear and conspicuous. That means your website disclaimer needs to be visible, noticeable, obvious and easily accessible on your website.

> FTC regulations require that disclaimers and disclosures must be clear and conspicuous.

The value of disclaimers depends upon the skill with which they are drafted. They need to be legally sound and customized based on the contents of the website. So, to use some disclaimer copied from another website or a generic form will turn out to be legally ineffective. It also can result in a claim of copyright infringement for using a disclaimer without permission. If you rely on some generalized disclaimer or borrow it from another practitioner's website to protect yourself, you may find that in an attempt to "save" money you have caused yourself to incur substantial losses.

RISK MANAGEMENT STRATEGIES

- Follow FTC rules and regulations regarding advertising and also comply with the consumer protection laws in your state. You can also become familiar with FTC regulations regarding testimonials by studying the FTC's Guides Concerning the Use of Endorsements and Testimonials in Advertising http:// www.ftc.gov/sites/default/files/attachments/press-releases/ftc-publishes-final-guides-governing-endorsements-testimonial s/091005revisedendorsementguides.pdf.
- If you are a non-licensed energy healing practitioner know, understand, and be in compliance with the laws and regulations in your state regarding licensed professions. For example, you do not want the description of your services on your website or in a client testimonial to be perceived as practicing

medicine, psychotherapy or another licensed profession. Avoiding this perception can protect you from being charged with the crime of practicing a licensed profession without a license.

- Obtain written permission from a client to use a testimonial. Licensed practitioners should research their regulations and rules to determine if they have requirements for testimonials. Some states do not allow licensed health care providers to use patient testimonials. Other states allow them but have specific requirements. For example, in New Jersey licensed clinical social workers must have a written and notarized permission agreement in order to use a patient's testimonial in marketing materials, including a website.

- Conduct a risk management audit of the contents of your website and other marketing materials. Make sure you have a legally sound website disclaimer drafted specifically for the contents of your website. A generic or borrowed website disclaimer will not protect you. The cost of engaging the services of a risk management consultant or lawyer who has the expertise in energy healing methods to help you with your website is an excellent investment.

Section VII

The Sacred Contract Between Practitioner and Client Archetypes as Guardians of Ethical Relationships

Introduction to the concept of Sacred Contracts

TRADITIONALLY, IN THOSE HEALTH CARE professions subject to state licensing laws and regulations, the orientation of ethics has focused on avoiding professional discipline and litigation. As a result, a licensing board's enforcement of unethical conduct by a licensed practitioner tends to be punitive in nature. Licensed practitioners can lose their license to practice, if they are brought up on charges of unprofessional conduct due to ethical violations. However, with the growing use of energy healing methods, the overall purpose of ethics codes is not punitive in nature. Instead the purpose of ethics codes is to guide practitioners so that the client's welfare remains the first priority. This orientation of ethics emphasizes that ethical conduct should be based on the values, motivations, and relationships energy healing practitioners share with their clients. Kylea Taylor, in her book The Ethics of Caring, has expanded the definition of ethics to include the spiritual principle of reverence for life, which underlies all healing systems. Taylor's expanded therapeutic paradigm is based on honoring the interconnectedness of all life in all dimensions. Taylor's model recognizes spiritual longings and psychospiritual phenomena as part of this expanded therapeutic paradigm (i.e. any state of consciousness in which there is heightened sensitivity and awareness and in which there can arise a variety of specific phenomena not usually recognized by traditional psychology (Taylor, 1995). This model is appropriate for understanding ethics in energy healing methods, because it takes into account the subtle energies and intuition that many of these modalities use in working with clients. This ethics of caring model can give practitioners insight into themselves and the sacred relationship they share with their clients. When I use the word "sacred," I am not referring to any religion. Instead "sacred" is meant to recognize and honor the interconnectedness we all share on the quantum level.

How do energy healing practitioners begin to create ethical relationships with themselves, their clients, and their community? I propose they structure them as sacred contracts. Framing your relationship with your clients as a sacred contract includes not only a commitment to ethical behavior but also working with clients within the field of the heart and creating multi-levels of awareness with them.

Caroline Myss, the author of *Sacred Contracts, Awakening Your Divine Potential*, gives practitioners a psychospiritual tool for understanding their life's mission in a way that makes the best use of their energy. When we are working well with our energy, taking responsibility for our actions, and making wise choices, we are also creating the best expression of our personal power. Our best expression means we are behaving ethically with integrity. Caroline Myss calls this living in accordance with our Sacred Contract. Myss developed her theory that each of us has a Sacred Contract after working for 17 years as a medical intuitive – someone who can intuitively "read" a person's internal physiological condition, rather than by physical examination and diagnosis.

She discovered in her work that most people yearn to know and understand what their mission is on earth. She realized that the details of how we live our lives can accumulate to create health or illness. The further we stray from our true mission in life, the more frustrated we can become. This can also result in our energy being more out of sync. After conducting thousands of readings, Myss came to the conclusion that a sacred organizing principle is shaping the energy within each of us. From this observation she developed the concept that each of us has a purpose in life as defined by our individual Sacred Contract. She then created a specific psychospiritual tool for deciphering our Sacred Contract.

A brief statement of Myss' definition of a Sacred Contract is the agreements we make with the Universe, Spirit, Source, or the Divine (whatever resonates with you personally) on a soul level, prior to coming into physical form, about the lessons we will learn and the relationships we will encounter for the purpose of evolving our soul. The ultimate goal of working with your Sacred Contract is spiritual transformation. Spiritual transformation results when you move from seeing things strictly in the physical, material terms to seeing there are reasons why things happen as they do, and that there is a greater plan behind them. Myss says, "As vital parts of a larger, universal Spirit, we each have been put here on earth to fulfill a Sacred Contract that enhances our personal spiritual growth while contributing to the evolution of the entire global soul" (Myss, 2001 p.4). Her basic assumption is that we are spiritual beings having a physical experience on earth. Therefore, we are on a spiritual journey by being here on earth. Part of our contract requires that we discover what it is that we are meant to do. Source, in return, promises to give us the guidance we need through our intuition, dreams, hunches, coincidences and other indicators. Our Sacred Contract is the guided plan for our life co-created by Spirit and us. It includes many individual agreements (subcontracts) to meet and work with certain people (Myss, 2001). I think this idea resonates with those of us who have gone into the healing professions because most have felt called to serve in this way. Many of us would acknowledge that a significant part of our personal Sacred Contract is to do healing work.

Ethics concerns the sacred or special relationship between practitioner and client. When we frame our relationships with our clients as a sacred contract, we lay the foundation for ethical behavior. By incorporating the sacred into our practices, we embrace the expanded definition of ethics to include reverence for all life. We honor the interconnectedness we have with our clients. In other words, we are in "right relationship" with them to use a Buddhist term.

The first material term of the sacred contract between practitioner and client is "to do no harm,". That means not only physical harm but also emotional, intellectual, energetic, and spiritual harm. This is especially applicable to practitioners who use energy healing methods with their clients. With a sacred contract as the guiding principle, the ethics of an energy healing practitioner are judged on all levels of awareness, including physical, emotional, intellectual, energetic, and spiritual. It's believed that acting in integrity is considered highly ethical behavior. Integrity means the practitioner's behavior is congruent with her values, knowledge, skills, intuition, and feelings. Integrity also means that there is harmonious, consensual dialogue between internal functions with results in external behavior that is consistent and ethical. (Taylor, 1995) In other words, acting in integrity means that you are in alignment with your own personal Sacred Contract. By being in alignment with your Sacred Contract, it also provides you with the opportunity to honor your relationships with your clients as sacred contracts.

This ethics of caring model goes beyond moral codes and can help practitioners be in service to their highest natures and to grow more in harmony with own their Sacred Contract. Morals change with the times, are different in various cultures, and are based on the judgments of the particular society. Spiritual truths do not vary with time. When we identify our relationship with our client as a sacred contract, then we are invoking spiritual truths as the governing force in our relationship with them.

Ethical guidelines within a particular profession can provide an external locus of control. It is advisable to use external guidelines when you choose a course of action with clients. In fact, it's mandatory if you are subject to a specific code of ethics within your profession This includes licensed practitioners that must follow a code of ethics and practitioners who are members in a professional organization that has a code of ethics.

However, when honoring the sacred contract with your client, you will drop down into a deeper level of awareness (i.e. heart space). You will use your own values and motivations in conjunction with external guidelines to choose a course of action. Self-examination of values and motivations stimulates development of an internal locus of control for those who want to expand their ethical consciousness (Taylor, 1995). Think of this internal locus of control as your own personal honor code for ethical behavior. Having a personal honor code as part of your sacred contract with regards to ethics is more important when working with clients intuitively and on an energetic level. Because working with clients in this manner can take the practitioner and client into uncharted territory where external guidelines may not be helpful.

When Myss developed her concept that each individual has a Sacred Contract, she concluded that each of us has a unique combination of twelve archetypal patterns or archetypes. These archetypes are our spiritual guides in understanding ourselves and work with us to support our personal development. Myss chose the number twelve because of its symbolic and mystical qualities that have had meaning in various cultures for centuries. For example, there are the twelve tribes of Israel, the twelve disciples of Jesus, the twelve houses of the zodiac in astrology, the twelve months of the year, and the twelve hours on a clock.

Myss believes four of these twelve archetypes are universal energetic patterns that we all share. They will be described in more detail below and how they impact the therapeutic relationship. The other eight archetypes are personal to each individual and part of the fun and challenge of discerning your Sacred Contract is to conduct a life review. This life reviews process helps to determine which archetypal patterns have been with you during your life. Of course, there are many archetypes that have been identified and numerous books have been written about them. Myss lists and describes about eighty archetypes in the appendix to her book for readers to study. These archetypes include ancient figures, such as the Goddess, Warrior, King, and Magician, or contemporary ones, such as the Networker, Environmentalist, Diva, and Protester.

> When we as caregivers are fluent in seeing archetypal patterns in ourselves and our clients, we create the framework for honoring the sacred contract between us.

About archetypes

ARCHETYPES ARE UNIVERSAL FORMS OF cosmic intelligence, dynamic living forms of energy that are shared in many people's thoughts and emotions, across cultures and countries. They form the symbolic, underlying principles that define the architecture of our lives, and speak to us in symbolic language. It's important to remember that archetypes are neutral and manifest energies from both light and shadow sides. An integral part of the therapeutic dynamic is to bring the shadow parts of us into the light so healing can occur. Carl Jung, the famous Swiss psychiatrist and psychologist, believed that archetypes live in the collective unconscious through which all souls are connected. He was the first to define and explore extensively the nature and role of universal archetypes in human consciousness. The work of archetypes implies that although they are energetic patterns of influence that are both ancient and universal, they become quite personalized when they are part of an individual's psyche (Myss, 2001).

Since a Sacred Contract is embodied in a support system of twelve archetypes, they become energy guides to each individual's highest potential. Knowledge of your archetypal patterns helps you understand why you have had certain relationships They can also help you understand why you have had to take on specific duties that either delighted you or seemed burdensome and destructive.

According to Myss, we all share four major archetypes, which symbolize our major life changes, and how we choose to survive in the physical world; the Child, the Victim, the Prostitute, and the Saboteur. All four archetypes influence how we relate to material power, how we respond to authority, and how we make choices. I believe that these four archetypes are active participants within the therapeutic relationship for both the practitioner and client. Within the context of using energy healing techniques, they are much more intense due to the nature of the work. Energy healing practitioners may move beyond the mere biographical realm into the transpersonal, intuitive, energetic, and quantum realms with clients. These archetypes then become amplified and can be active energetic patterns in the healing process.

Therefore, it is advisable for practitioners to be conscious of the energetic dynamics of these four principal archetypes within their own psyches as well as their clients. For practitioners, these survival archetypes need to be stable and actualized in order to lay the foundation for ethical decision making with clients. They can support the practitioner's spiritual maturity and life mission (i.e. Sacred Contract). We will explore each of these survival archetypes as they relate to the therapeutic setting that incorporates energy healing methods . Although there are different interpretations that can be presented about these archetypes, for the purposes of our discussion, I am using Myss' orientation, as set forth in her book.

The four major archetypes

Child archetype

The Child archetype is the guardian of innocence and is among the most powerful patterns in our psyches. It is our first stage of consciousness. There are many manifestations of the Child archetype, such as the Orphaned Child, the Wounded Child, the Natural Child, the Needy Child, the Magical Child, and so forth. Numerous therapeutic models work with the Child archetype as a tool for healing and growth. There have also been many self-help books written about engaging our inner child. As a result of this emphasis on our inner child, our society is very familiar with the Child archetype. The Child archetype is central in understanding the dynamics of power in the therapeutic relationship. As stated in Section II, being sensitive to the power differential is considered one of the core ethical concepts in therapeutic relationships.

In theory and in ethical practice, awareness of the power differential serves to bring benefit to the client who is in a more vulnerable position. The power differential is inherent in any therapeutic relationship. There is an implicit acknowledgment that the practitioner has more knowledge and expertise in this area than the client. This is amplified by the physical, psychological, and transpersonal aspects of innovative energy healing modalities. Because of the power differential, the client is disposed to respond to the practitioner as he does to other authority figures. In doing so, the client engages his Child archetype and may bring to the session any unconscious or unresolved issues applicable to this energetic pattern. Professional healing relationships usually have strong transference elements in which the parent-child archetypal pattern is unconsciously re-established.

If the child archetype is activated in the therapeutic relationship, the client can transfer to the practitioner the client's unresolved needs, feelings, and issues from childhood. The client reacts unconsciously to the practitioner's feelings, thoughts, expectations, and beliefs and may project his own feelings, thoughts, expectations, and behavior onto the practitioner. Energy healing methods create space for profound healing to take place but can also make the client more vulnerable and fragile. The practitioner who is aware of the energies and dynamics of the client's Child archetype will be able to maintain clear boundaries and correctly handle the power differential. In addition, the practitioner who is skilled in working with a client's Child archetype creates a sacred, safe place and an ethic of caring for the client.

Victim archetype

The Victim archetype is the guardian of self-esteem and personal boundaries. The primary objective is to develop positive self-esteem and personal power by interacting with people through acts of honesty, integrity, courage, and self-respect. Being a victim is a common fear, and we all experience various situations where we face that fear. Hopefully, through these experiences, which can be very difficult, we learn to set boundaries for ourselves. The Victim archetype puts us on alert whenever we feel like we are being victimized. It teaches us to empower ourselves and take responsibility for our independence.

As stated before, energy healing methods can place the client in a more vulnerable position during sessions when deeply buried trauma may be unearthed. This entry into the unconscious realms of the client can create opportunities for the power differential to shift in a way that may activate both the client's Victim archetype as well as the practitioner's Victim archetype. If the practitioner has a conscious or unconscious personal longing to be the magical healer, and the client attributes her healing process to the magical healing qualities of the, the client becomes disempowered. If the practitioner accepts this transference, it can create a co-dependency and activate the client's Victim archetype.

In addition, the practitioner may bring the archetypal pattern described as the Karpman Drama Triangle into the therapeutic process (Karpman, S.B. (1968). *Fairy tales and script drama analysis.* Transactional Analysis Bulletin. 7(27) 39-43 in James M & Jongeward, D. [1971]. Born to win). In the Karpman Drama Triangle, there are three interchangeable archetypes, the Rescuer, Persecutor, and Victim. If the practitioner is engaged with the Rescuer archetype, by bringing the magical rescuing words to the client, then the client is engaged with the Victim archetype because she has disempowered herself. The client discounts her own inner wisdom, internal magician, and healer, when she projects the role outside herself onto her practitioner. This can result in the client feeling betrayed by the practitioner because the practitioner accepted the projection and did not return it at once. In effect, she did not say, "this is not mine; the Magician/Healer archetype is part of you." Because the practitioner has kept what is not hers and has thereby disempowered the client, she has switched from engaging the Rescuer archetype to engaging the Persecutor archetype. The client may realize at some point that the practitioner has not acted in the client's best interests. Instead the practitioner has acted out of the practitioner's own need to be seen as a gifted healer. When she realizes this, the client may take on the role of the Persecutor archetype, activating the practitioner's Victim archetype by leaving the practitioner vulnerable to charges of unethical behavior (Taylor, 1995) and a possible lawsuit.

By being aware of this drama triangle pattern, practitioners may keep themselves from jumping too quickly into the role of rescuer and all-knowing healer. When fully actualized, the Victim archetype represents the strength of good personal boundaries and positive self-esteem. These qualities are essential for energy healing practitioners wanting to behave ethically with integrity and offer the highest level of service to their clients.

Prostitute archetype

The Prostitute archetype is the guardian of faith. The core issue is how much are you willing to sell yourself – your morals, your integrity, your intellect, your word, your body, your soul, for the sake of physical security. The Prostitute archetype is the ally who puts you on alert every time you contemplate shifting your faith from the spiritual to the physical. We most often see an active Prostitute archetype in people who stay in bad marriages or in miserable jobs only because of financial issues. The therapeutic relationship is fertile ground for the practitioner to engage in the shadow side of the Prostitute archetype, as well as to develop the positive side. For example, the shadow aspect of the Prostitute archetype is present if the practitioner continues to see a client only because he does not want to lose the income. The shadow aspect of the Prostitute archetype may also be activated if the practitioner mainly works with a client because the practitioner gets an ego boost from having a prominent client. The positive side of the Prostitute archetype is engaged when the practitioner has made a commitment to the highest ethical standards of service to his clients. When this occurs, the Prostitute archetype becomes one of his best allies in honoring the sacred contract between the practitioner and client.

Saboteur archetype

The Saboteur archetype is the guardian of choice. The core issue for the Saboteur is fear of inviting change into one's life, change that requires responding in a positive way to opportunities to shape and deepen one's spirit. The Saboteur archetype can be silenced with acts of courage and by following intuitive guidance. The choice to respond to our intuition can rearrange our familiar world. We all know the voice of our inner saboteur. It's the voice that tells us we are not good enough or that we can't possibly take that job. We also know what it is like to be sabotaged by others in our personal relationships and in the workplace.

The Saboteur archetype, as the guardian of choices, is also highly active in the therapeutic relationship. Many energy healing methods involve some degree of non-ordinary states of consciousness. Fundamentally healing is about change and profound change can involve a radical shift in self-view, world view, and spiritual understanding. A client experiencing an energy healing method can experience a rush of emotion, have greater vulnerability, and be disoriented. It takes the client out of the dullness of ordinary life and allows a deeper awareness to emerge. Energy healing methods can create openings in clients for awareness, change, and growth. Clients are usually aware of the process they are undergoing and, in some sense, welcome the awareness of the change that is happening.

The practitioner can use the power of his or her position in the therapeutic relationship to provide permission for the client to embrace the positive aspects of the Saboteur archetype This is especially the case when the client feels hesitant to go beyond what he knows. Energy psychology talks about this phenomenon as a psychological reversal termed an "identity reversal." A practitioner can treat this reversal and offer protection when the client feels fear in response to the change happening in the client's life as a result of energy work. Of course, the practitioner needs to have done her own healing work so she can be a lamp bearer for the client traveling in uncharted and sometimes frightening territory. She needs to have faced her fears of change and spiritual growth with the assistance of her own Saboteur archetype.

Other archetypal patterns

In addition to the four major archetypes discussed above, a number of archetypal energies can also significantly impact the therapeutic relationship with clients. Under Myss' model, our Sacred Contract includes the four major archetypes discussed above and an additional eight other primary archetypes. When a practitioner is astute in recognizing these additional primary archetypes in clients, it can honor and support the sacred contract between them. Here are a few archetypal patterns that can impact the therapeutic relationship.

Healer archetype

One archetype that is prevalent in those who engage in energy healing work is the Healer. The Healer archetype manifests in those who have a passion to serve others in the form of repairing body, mind, and spirit. It expresses itself through channels other than those classically associated with healing of illnesses. It's important to look beyond the occupations of nurse, doctor, massage therapist, counselor or psychologist. You can be strongly guided by this archetype in any occupation or role in life. Some people, by their very nature, personal vibration, and personality are able to inspire others to release their painful histories or make changes in their lives that redirect the course of their future. Myss says that one of the essential characteristics of the Healer archetype is the inherent strength and ability to assist people in transforming their pain into a healing process. An additional characteristic is having the "wiring" to channel energy needed to generate physical, emotional, and spiritual changes. The shadow aspect of the Healer archetype can manifest through a desire to take advantage of those who need help. Another shadow aspect would be if a practitioner makes claims that he can heal the client from whatever ailment of illness the client may have. It can also manifest if the practitioner fails to care for herself (Myss, 2001).

Rescuer & Servant archetypes

It is not uncommon for someone to believe they carry the energy pattern of the Healer archetype when, in fact, they have the Rescuer or Servant archetype. The Rescuer provides strength and support to others in crisis. If a practitioner is attuned with the Rescuer archetype, then it's essential for the practitioner to establish healthy boundaries with clients. The practitioner would need to be alert to the shadow side of the Rescuer archetype – doing too much for the client, thereby disempowering the client and making him or her dependent on the practitioner. Not maintaining healthy boundaries can result in co-dependency issues with clients. An extreme example would be if the practitioner had a client live with her. Situations engaging the shadow side of the Rescuer archetype can lead to ethical violations and potential legal claims.

The Servant archetype engages aspects of the psyche that call one to make oneself available for the benefit and enhancement of the lives of others. This may include spiritual or healing services to others. If this archetype resonates as part of your healing practice, then it is important to maintain your own well-being. Otherwise, it is easy to lose focus by becoming consumed by the needs of your clients. This self-neglect can trigger unethical behavior by diffusing boundaries between the practitioner and client. This can trigger issues of transference and countertransference.

Mother, Father, and Lover archetypes

In using energy healing methods with clients, it's possible for the client to develop strong needs for nurturing, sexual contact, and spiritual connection. The potential for transference can be enhanced due to the personal desires and spiritual longings of the client. Also, the potential for countertransference can be enhanced due to the personal desires and spiritual longings of the practitioner. For example, a practitioner may discern that a client carries the archetypal pattern of the abandoned child. As a result, the client has a personal desire for maternal nurturing. The practitioner needs to be careful with how the practitioner "nurtures" the client. Clear boundaries would need be honored by the practitioner in order to not exploit the client. If the practitioner carries the archetypal pattern of the Lover, the practitioner would need to be vigilant not to cross into unethical territory around sexual contact with a client. These powerful archetypal patterns can result in client projections onto the practitioner, ranging from the divine to the demonic. This can bring confusion, boundary issues, and ethical violations to the therapeutic setting.

Damsel archetype

There are an infinite number of archetypal patterns that may be active in the therapeutic relationship, especially when working with energy healing models. The practitioner dedicated to honoring the sacred contract with his clients, will observe and be sensitive to archetypal patterns active within the therapeutic relationship for both parties. For example, a client may carry the Damsel archetype, wanting the practitioner to save her while projecting a romantic illusion onto the practitioner. A practitioner who recognizes these energies will inspire the client to rely on herself to be the rescuer and the catalyst for her own empowerment.

Judge archetype

A practitioner that carries a Judge archetype will need to be vigilant to not judge the client or try to control the session, but instead to allow the inner healer of the client to be present and a directive force in the healing process.

Slave archetype

The practitioner who has a client with a Slave archetype will need to pay attention to make sure the client doesn't surrender his authority to the practitioner as an external authority figure out of fear of making his own choices.

Don Juan archetype

If either party to the therapeutic sacred contract carries the seductive energy of the Don Juan archetype, then boundaries, especially around touch will be a significant ethical concern of the practitioner.

Vampire archetype

At some time, almost every practitioner will encounter a client who exhibits behavior that can be described as co-dependent. Co-dependent behavior can reflect the energetic pattern of the Vampire archetype. These clients tend to be needy, hold on to relationships that are unhealthy, and they can be chronic complainers. If during or after a session with a client, you feel drained energetically, physically, emotionally or mentally, you are most likely encountering the

Vampire archetype. If a client exhibits the shadow side the Vampire archetype, the practitioner must pay careful attention to boundaries and be vigilant about managing the power differential.

Whether or not you choose to believe in Myss' concept, identifying, observing, honoring, and working with the archetypal patterns within your psyche, as well as your clients, can help you develop an ethical practice. It can also provide a solid foundation for you to be able to honor the sacred contract between you and your clients. In creating ethical relationships with clients, ourselves, and our communities, understanding the dynamic nature of archetypal patterns, with a deep understanding of the light and shadow sides of archetypes, is an invaluable tool.

Expanding the therapeutic paradigm

INNOVATIVE ENERGY HEALING METHODS CAN expand the therapeutic paradigm beyond the biographical domain of the client to include transpersonal experiences (experiences beyond the personal identity, physical reality, and causal relationships of the client). The archetypes reside in this transpersonal realm. Consequently, by their nature, innovative energy healing methods can include archetypes as active participants in the therapeutic relationship. In addition, this expanded therapeutic paradigm can include personal myth which goes beyond the notion that it either happened or it did not from a strictly biographical standpoint. Personal myth can also intimately involve archetypes as partners in the healing process. Personal myths are not fantasy but rather a story constructed symbolically with archetypes that represents factual reality. Therefore, from an ethical standpoint it is imperative that the practitioner have the expertise and requisite training to assist his/her clients.

The openness of the practitioner is a key factor in how normal a client feels when having archetypal, transpersonal, or mythic experiences as part of the therapeutic process. Another key factor is for the practitioner to support the client in allowing these experiences to develop and amplify as part of the healing journey. Mary Sykes Wylie writes "Blind allegiance to a particular therapeutic model becomes an ethical failing when the therapist consistently gives more weight to the model than to what the clients say they want and need" (Wylie, M.S. (Mar/Apr, 1989) The ethical therapist: looking for fence posts The Family Therapy Networker, Washington, D.C.26.). This openness is an important aspect of the sacred contract between practitioner and client. It can enable the practitioner to stay present for and to accept the client's archetypal, transpersonal, and mythic experiences, as well as the usual biographical ones.

Integrating the energy healing experience

ANOTHER ESSENTIAL TERM OF THE sacred contract between practitioner and client is for the practitioner to affirm the archetypal, transpersonal, or mythic reality her client may have experienced. In addition, the practitioner needs to prepare the client for the possibility of rejection of her new "reality" by her social system. It is an ethical failing not to assist clients in integrating their energy healing experiences into their everyday lives.

Spiritually aware practitioners who honor and recognize the sacredness of the therapeutic relationship have a deep longing to use any spiritual power they have ethically, with integrity and discernment. They strive to conduct themselves in accordance with the sacred contract they share with their clients.

Section VIII

Sample Ethical Guidelines and Ethics Codes

The importance of national organizations and ethical guidelines

A PROFESSIONAL ORGANIZATION CAN SET the tone of valuing the specific energy healing method for its practitioners. It can create certification programs and present conferences for educational and training purposes. Organizations can provide continuing education and training regarding ethical and legal issues that arise in working with clients using energy healing methods. An organization can unite to defend its ethics and the efficacy of a particular healing modality. As stated previously, energy healing methods are still considered on the fringe of the mainstream health care industry. It can be illegal and considered unethical to practice an innovative energy healing method with a client unless that method has proven value. Practitioners of that method may not be able to demonstrate therapeutic value by competent and reliable scientific research. They can't make the argument that the method has been accepted by a critical mass of traditionally licensed professionals. One of the purposes that formal organizations serve is to demonstrate that a particular energy healing method is effective for healing or personal/spiritual growth and exploration. The organization has numbers of members (practitioners and clients) who agree there is therapeutic value in the method. The organization can proceed to create ethical guidelines. By doing so, the organization is in a better position to defend its method if its practices should be questioned by regulatory agencies or the legal system. Creating ethical guidelines are important because when something is written down in our culture, it gains credibility. Written ethics codes describe the values of the organization, and publishing them reminds the membership and others about the integrity of the organization.

It's helpful to be aware of ethics codes that have been developed for energy healing methods. Below you will find sample ethical guidelines from Matrix Energetics International, Inc., which I developed for the Matrix Energetics Practitioner Certification Program. Following the Matrix Energetics Ethical Guidelines, you will find the Code of Ethics for the Healing Touch Program. These are being provided to you as samples so that you have an idea about the ethical guidelines and code of ethics that have been developed by these two organizations.

Matrix Energetics ® Ethical Guidelines

1. Practitioners hold as the highest priority for their professional activities the health and welfare of their clients and others with whom they become professionally involved.

2. Practitioners are committed to first do no harm and to use intuition with integrity to avoid manipulating clients or projecting their own issues onto clients.

3. Practitioners provide a safe, clean, welcoming, supportive, appropriate, professional and comfortable environment for their services that supports healing.

4. Practitioners agree to use Matrix Energetics only in accordance with the standards of practice set by MEI as developed by Dr. Richard Bartlett.

5. Practitioners understand the importance of doing their own personal growth work as it relates to ethical behavior with colleagues and clients. Practitioners are fully committed to personal integrity, authenticity and their ongoing commitment to healing and lifelong personal development.

6. Practitioners strive for professional excellence through ongoing assessment of personal strengths, limitations, and effectiveness and understand their own limitations as caregivers.

7. Practitioners conduct business and professional activities with integrity, in a professional, honest, and fair manner.

8. Practitioners abide by the applicable local, state, and national laws, regulations, and rules that govern the delivery of their health care and healing services.

9. Practitioners seek feedback, consultation, guidance and supervision from colleagues, mentors, and supervisors to help them deal with ethical issues, blind spots and shadow behavior that could create ethical vulnerabilities in working with clients.

10. Practitioners have developed and are able to articulate their own personal code of ethics, which is compatible with these Ethical Guidelines. Practitioners recognize that a fully developed personal code of ethics code will guide and assist them in situations where written ethical guidelines do not provide specific instructions in working with clients.

11. Practitioners are clear enough about their limitations both personally and professionally, to know when to refer a client to another health care practitioner. Practitioners maintain a referral list consisting of high caliber and ethical colleagues in order to comply with this ethical guideline to refer clients when appropriate.

12. Practitioners perform only those services for which they are qualified, accurately representing their education, certifications, licensure, professional affiliations and other qualification. Practitioners only perform their services within their legally defined scope of practice.

13. Practitioners do not diagnose, prescribe, or treat any medical or psychological disorder unless licensed and credentialed to do so under applicable laws.

14. Practitioners remain up-to-date on the latest developments in theory and research concerning Matrix Energetics. They pursue continuous professional development and continuing education.

15. Practitioners obtain informed consent from clients and provide clear and accurate information to prospective clients. Clients must be informed that Matrix Energetics is still considered novel and experimental, and that as consumers, they have the right to know about and use mainstream treatments that are also used to treat their presenting issue. Any claims made by a Practitioner concerning the efficacy of Matrix Energetics must be substantiated and presented within a theoretical framework.

16. Practitioners discuss with clients in advance the limitations and the risks and benefits associated with the services they provide to their clients.

17. Practitioners always put the needs of their clients first and foremost, treating them with compassion and establishing a collaborative relationship with those they serve. Practitioners do not promise or guarantee any particular results when working with any client nor do they aggrandize themselves or dramatize their abilities to perceive or work with Matrix Energetics.

18. Practitioners maintain confidentiality within the therapeutic relationship with clients and respect each client's right to privacy. Practitioners understand and inform their clients about the legal limits of confidentiality and privilege according to each practitioner's licensure or non-licensure status.

19. Practitioners recognize that in dealing with a client's energy system, they have a higher level of responsibility to be aware of and tend to subtle boundary issues and

must establish and maintain proper boundaries with clients. Practitioners do not use their abilities to work with energy to exploit the power differential between themselves and their clients.

20. It is never acceptable for a Practitioner to develop a new friendship, business relationship or any kind of romantic/sexual relationship with a client while treatment is occurring, and a Practitioner must avoid dual relationships that might negatively impact the effectiveness of their services. If a Practitioner is a licensed health care provider, then such Practitioner is subject to the laws and regulations that such Practitioner must comply with under their applicable licensure applicable to dual relationships and those laws and regulations supersede this guideline.

21. Practitioners are sensitive to a client's feelings about being touched, discuss those feelings as appropriate, and gain permission before applying any procedure that requires touch.

22. Practitioners recognize the pitfalls of being overly attached to the outcomes of the services they provide and understand that such attachment is detrimental to the healing process.

23. Practitioners treat all colleagues with dignity, respect and courtesy, talk about colleagues in respectful and appreciative ways and credit colleagues for their contributions and innovations.

24. Practitioners keep written records as appropriate to their professional function and setting.

25. Practitioners do not make misleading, false, deceptive, or fraudulent statements concerning 1) their training, experience, education, credentials or competence; 2) their services; or 3) any claims of curative ability regarding the Matrix Energetics System.

HEALING TOUCH PROGRAM CODE OF ETHICS

PURPOSE: The purpose of the following Code of Ethics is to guide the therapeutic practice of Healing Touch.

DEFINITION HEALING TOUCH: Healing Touch is an energy therapy in which practitioners consciously use their hands in a heart centered and intentional way to enhance, support and facilitate physical, emotional, mental and spiritual health and self-healing. Healing Touch utilizes light or near-body touch to clear, balance and energize the human energy system in an effort to promote healing for the whole person; mind, body, spirit.

GOAL: The goal of Healing Touch is to restore harmony and balance in the energy system, creating an optimal environment for the body's natural and innate tendency to move toward self-healing.

1: **Scope of Practice** Healing Touch practitioners use Healing Touch within the scope of their background, current licensing and credentialing. They represent themselves to the public in accordance with their credentials. They practice within the guidelines of this Code of Ethics; the Healing Touch Program's Scope of Practice statement; and state, local and federal laws and regulations.

2: **Collaborative Care** Healing Touch is a complementary energy therapy which can be used in conjunction with traditional therapies or as a sole modality. Practitioners know the limits of their professional competence and do not step beyond these boundaries. They do not diagnose, prescribe, or treat medical conditions or disorders unless they hold a license which permits them to do so. They are credentialed and in good standing with their respective/ legal licensing or credentialing body/bodies. Appropriate referrals to other health care professionals are made when necessary.

3: **Intention** Healing Touch is used to promote the well-being and healing for each client. Client safety, educational needs, and well-being are safeguarded by the practitioner. Practitioners working with subtle energies are careful to use their ability only in a manner beneficial to the client. Instead of trying to change the client in any way, practitioners use their intentionality to cooperate "with the field, the emerging order" (Watson, 2005). They use their abilities with humility, consciousness and professionalism.

4: **Principles of Healing** Healing Touch practitioners know that healing is a personal, individualized process that occurs from within the inner dimensions of the client. The client is supported by the HT Practitioner in self-directing this sacred process. The HT practitioner creates a conscious, reverent, caring-healing environment. Practitioners foster an optimal condition for that client to remember and move toward their wholeness through the steps of the HT Sequence and the practitioner-client relationship.

5: **Respectful Care Healing** Touch practitioners maintain high standards of professionalism in their care. They treat clients and colleagues with respect, courtesy, care and consideration. HT practitioners respect their client's individuality, beliefs, inherent worth, and dignity. They respect the client's right to be involved in their treatment and they empower the client to give feedback, alter or discontinue the session at any time. Practitioners provide information that assists clients in making informed decisions about their care.

6: **Equality and Acceptance** Healing Touch practitioners work in partnership with the client to promote healing regardless of race, creed, color, age, gender, sexual orientation, politics or social status, spiritual practice or health condition. The client's inner process, spiritual practices and pacing of healing are respected and supported. No specific religious/spiritual belief or practice is promoted in Healing Touch.

7: **Creating a Healing Environment** Healing Touch is provided in a variety of environments. Practitioners provide (when possible) a private, safe environment conducive to healing in which the client can relax and be receptive to the healing process. Safe and clear professional boundaries are described and maintained. Permission for receiving Healing Touch is obtained through the informed consent process. Where hands-on touch is appropriate for the healing process, it is non-sexual, gentle and within the client's consent and boundaries. The client is fully dressed except in medical situations, or other professional therapies requiring disrobing, in which case appropriate draping is used.

8: **Healing Touch Sequence** The Healing Touch practitioner uses the ten-step process as a foundation and guideline, for administration of the work and in documentation. The ten steps are: (1) Intake/Update; (2) Practitioner Preparation; (3) Pre-treatment Energetic Assessment; (4) Identification of Health Issues/ Problem Statements; (5) Mutual Goals and Intention for Healing; (6) Healing Touch Interventions; (7) Post-treatment Energetic Assessment; (8) Ground and Release; (9) Evaluation, and (10) Treatment Plan. Sequential order of the ten steps may vary depending on the specific situation, methods administered and flow of the session.

9: **Disclosure and Education** Information is provided to the client on an individualized basis taking into account expressed needs and personal situations. The Practitioner informs the client of her/his educational and experiential background in Healing Touch and any other related credentials they hold. They also provide an explanation of the treatment to the level of client's understanding, and clearly and accurately inform clients of the nature and terms of the service. The Practitioner discusses the HT treatment process as well as any relevant limitations or issues before HT interventions begin. Practitioners supply resources and/or additional materials that may support the client.

10: **Confidentiality** Client confidentiality is protected at all times and records are kept in a secure and private place in accordance with state and federal regulations. The Practitioner also informs clients of exceptions to their confidentiality such as disclosure for legal and regulatory requirements or to prevent eminent harm or danger to client or others. Client health information and treatment findings are documented appropriately and are specific to the practitioner's background and setting. Information is shared only with client's written permission.

11: **Legalities** Healing Touch practitioners are expected to understand and comply with the laws of the state(s) in which they are offering Healing Touch as well as applicable federal regulations in regards to obtaining or maintaining a license to touch. Those that have a professional license are expected to understand how touch either is or is not included or restricted in their scope of practice and comply accordingly. It is expected that HT Practitioners will carry liability/malpractice insurance according to state, federal and professional laws to protect themselves and clients. It is expected that HT Practitioners will maintain the appropriate business licenses according to their state requirements.

12: **Self-Development** Healing Touch practitioners practice self-care to enhance their own personal health in order to provide optimal care for others. They practice from a theoretical and experiential knowledge base as they continue to deepen their understanding of healing, the biofield, spiritual development, and personal evolution. They keep themselves current in the practice and research of Healing Touch and related areas and seek to continually expand their effectiveness as a practitioner.

13: **Professional Responsibility** Practitioners represent Healing Touch in a professional manner by exercising good judgment, practicing with integrity, and adhering to this Code of

Ethics and the HTP Scope of Practice. They encourage ethical behavior, by words and actions, to all parties. They consult a supervisor, HT mentor, HT instructor or Healing Touch Program Director when an unresolved ethical issue occurs.

Conclusion

It is the author's hope that you have gained a better understanding about the ethical and legal issues applicable to the practice of energy healing methods. Examining your values and behavior as they relate to your personal life and your professional practice can provide insights into areas of potential vulnerability that you may not have previously considered. Self-accountability is the cornerstone of ethical behavior. By implementing appropriate risk management strategies, you protect your practice and empower yourself to go out into the world and do your energy healing work.

Next Step After Reading This Book

Reading this book is the first step in gaining knowledge and understanding about practicing energy healing in integrity and experiencing the joy of offering your gifts legally and ethically. It demonstrates you are committed to bringing the highest ethical standards to your energy healing practice. What's the next step? I encourage you to earn a Certificate of Completion by taking the Exam based on the information in this book. Why? By earning your Certificate of Completion, you have demonstrated you have acquired an understanding and level of competency in ethics, legal issues, and risk management strategies in the practice of energy healing methods.

The Certificate of Completion is a professional credential that you do not acquire by reading this book. Here are some reasons why a Certificate of Completion is a valuable credential for your energy healing practice and worth the additional investment:

- It's required in order to become certified by the National Certification Center of Energy Practitioners.

- It can increase your client base. As energy healing grows in popularity people will be searching for energy healing practitioners with the best credentials and having training in ethics can put a star by your name.

- It can increase employment opportunities. As energy healing methods begin to become more integrated into mainstream health care, having training in ethics can put you at the top of the list for expanded practice opportunities.

- It can protect you if you are questioned by a licensing board, regulatory agency, or court of law. A licensing board won't take into account that you read a book but it will take into account your Certificate of Completion as evidence that you have had training in ethics and legal issues.

- It can provide you with continuing education hours in ethics.

Please give consideration to taking my Exam which is contains multiple choice questions and a few fill-in questions. By reading this book you will already have the knowledge and information needed to take successfully pass the test. You can purchase the Exam at www.midgemurphy.com.

References

1. Benjamin B, Sohnen-Moe, C. *The Ethics of Touch*, Tucson, AZ: SMA, 2003

2. Burkhardt, M. "Spirituality: An Analysis of the Concept," Holistic Nursing Practice, May 1989:60-77)

3. Cohen MH. *Complementary and Alternative Medicine: Legal Boundaries and Regulatory Perspectives*. Baltimore, MD: Johns Hopkins University Press, 1998.

4. Cohen MH. *Beyond Complementary Medicine: Legal and Ethical Perspectives on Health Care and Human Evolution*. Ann Arbor, MI: University of Michigan Press, 2000.

5. Cohen MH. *Future Medicine: Ethical Dilemmas, Regulatory Challenges, and Therapeutic Pathways to Health and Human Healing in Human Transformation*. Ann Arbor, MI: University of Michigan Press; 2003.

6. Eisenberg DM, et al. (1998) "Trends in alternative medicine use in the United States, 1990-1997" Journal of the American Medicine Association 280(18) 1569-1575.

7. Hover-Kramer D., Murphy, M. *Creating Right Relationship: a practical guide to ethics in energy therapies*. Eugene, OR: Territorial Publishing, 2005.

8. Karpman, S.B. (1968) "Fairy tales and script drama analysis," Transactional Analysis Bulletin, 7:27, 39-43. Also discussed in James, M. * Jongeward, D. (1973) Born to win, Reading MA: Addison-Wesley Publishing Company.

9. Myss, C (2001) *Sacred Contracts*, New, NY: Harmony Books

10. Schouten R & Cohen MH. "Legal issues in integration of complementary therapies into cardiology". In: Frishman WH, Weintraub MI, Micozzi MS, editors. Complementary and Integrative Therapies for Cardiovascular Disease (Elsevier, 2004); pp.20-55.

11. Taylor, K. (1995) *The Ethics of Caring*. Santa Cruz: Hanford Mead Publishers.

Additional Resources

Complementary and Alternative Medicine Law Blog by Michael
  H. Cohen www.camlawblog.com
Midge Murphy, JD, Ph.D. (energy medicine)
  Professional Liability Risk Management Consultant,
  www.midgemurphy.com
Ethics Handbook for Energy Healing Practitioners by David Feinstein
  & Donna Eden

Contact Information

Midge Murphy, JD, Ph.D. (Energy Medicine)
Professional Liability Risk Management Consultant
Ethics & Legal Principles in Energy Healing Methods
82985 Territorial Hwy, Eugene, OR 97405
www.midgemurphy.com

Made in the USA
Coppell, TX
30 September 2021

63278349R00095